WORKIN
THE HEART

WORKING FROM THE HEART

A Therapist's Guide to Heart-Centered Psychotherapy

William P. Ryan, PhD

JASON ARONSON
Lanham • Boulder • New York • Toronto • Plymouth, UK

Published by Jason Aronson
A wholly owned subsidary of Rowman & Littlefield
4501 Forbes Boulevard, Suite 200, Lanham, Maryland 20706
www.rowman.com

10 Thornbury Road, Plymouth PL6 7PP, United Kingdom

British Library Cataloguing in Publication Information Available

Library of Congress Cataloging-in-Publication Data
Ryan, William P., 1942-
Working from the heart : a therapists guide to heart-centered psychotherapy / William P. Ryan.
  p. ; cm.
1. Psychotherapy. I. Title.
[DNLM: 1. Psychotherapy—methods. 2. Love. 3. Professional-Patient Relations. WM 420]
RC480.R89 2011
616.89'14—dc22

                                        2011009966

ISBN 978-0-7657-0796-3 (cloth   )
ISBN 978-1-4422-3512-0 (pbk.   )
ISBN 978-0-7657-0798-7 (electronic)

To Jeanne, my companion
on the excellent adventure
of our journey together.

CONTENTS

ACKNOWLEDGMENTS

I know that authors usually wait until the end of their acknowledgements to express their gratitude for the loving support of their spouse. However, my sweetheart, Jeanne Lightfoot, has contributed to this book in such an extraordinary way that I want to honor her before anyone else. Jeanne was my most reliable source of support and biggest cheerleader throughout the several years of writing this very personal book. More importantly, she gave up over a year of time she would ordinarily have spent in her studio nurturing her own creativity to be my creative editor in the crafting of this manuscript. As fellow psychotherapists we have shared many deep conversations about our work over many years of morning coffee and evening chats. As a result she is very familiar with my ideas and how I talk about them. As a gifted editor she knew how to capture my voice in a clear and cogent way. After she had rephrased and reworked some of my material Jeanne would read it aloud to me. At those moments it would sound to me like what I had originally written. Yet I knew that she had performed her magic. What an extraordinary blessing it is to have someone who loves me deeply and knows me so well to be my primary editor. There are no words that can describe the depth of my gratefulness to you, my sweetheart.

For a year I met in a writing group with my dear friends and colleagues Jonathan Diamond and Molly Scott. Each of us was working on a book project. With just the right mixture of encouragement and challenge they helped me take the nascent ideas and shape them into an excellent proposal ready to send to publishers. Huge hugs of gratitude go out to Jon and Molly.

Then Julie Kirsch from Jason Aronson showed up to be just the right editor for this book. Because *Working From the Heart* is written in a nonacademic, somewhat informal and more personal style, it needed an acquisitions editor who would "get" that the voice fit the central themes of the book and also made it more accessible to a wide range of readers. Midway through the most intensive period of writing I became anxious that the publisher would be concerned about some of the more controversial chapters, so I sent Julie two additional chapters. She responded so positively that I was quickly reassured. A large hug to Julie.

In the last mile of the marathon Julie was promoted and Samantha Kirk took on the important task of getting the book to the finish line. Thank you Samantha.

I am also profoundly grateful to my patients for their willingness to let me tell their stories and, more importantly, for their valuing of and receptiveness of my way of being their therapist. Of course, out of respect for their privacy, I have changed names and details of their stories.

All of my initial drafts and subsequent rewrites were handwritten on yellow legal pads. A giant hug to Lorena Loubsky for her ability to decipher my writing and her perseverance in getting my words onto her computer.

Grateful hugs also go to my sons Mark, Scott, Chris, and John for their ongoing interest and support during the years of working on this book.

INTRODUCTION

I love my patients. It may be a kind of heresy in the current climate of behavioral objectives and short-term outcomes required by managed care to say that the love of the therapist for the patient is one of the most important aspects of psychotherapeutic work. Yet that is indeed what I am saying. Love is not measurable. Love is not concrete, rational or linear. Yet our patients experience it in ways that are palpable. In psychological research, whenever patients are asked to evaluate what was most helpful to them in producing a successful outcome in therapy, invariably they say, "My therapist really cared about me as a person."

My psychotherapeutic approach is not unique or revolutionary. I am not saying that all patients need is love, or that we should ignore justifiable concerns about boundary issues. What I am advocating is a shift in the figure-ground. Most of the therapists I know are compassionate and caring people. When we entered this field, we had a heartfelt desire to help people with their problems and suffering. Our training pushed that into the background and emphasized theory, technique and professional distance. I am suggesting that it is time to bring compassionate caring into the foreground. It is not that techniques and theories should go into the background, but rather that a synthesis needs to occur. Patients benefit not only from our minds, but also from our hearts. When we work in a heart-centered way, we feel freer to be both professionals and loving human beings. I do not consider this a revolution, but rather an evolution.

At the age of sixty-nine, after thirty-five years of private practice, I am an elder in the field of psychotherapy. Five years ago, I was diagnosed with a very aggressive cancer. After the surgeon removed my spleen, a fist-sized organ, he said that it weighed eight pounds and looked like a deflated basketball. As a survivor, I do not know when or if the cancer will return. Yet I am very acutely aware that my allotted time is limited. Each day I ponder the question, *What do I want to do with my time?* One persistent response is that I want to leave a legacy to the therapists who come after me. I want to pass on what I have learned about effective psychotherapy that they may not hear from other teachers or read in other books.

Most specifically, I want to advocate that therapists develop a more heart-centered approach to our work. From my perspective, the love of the therapist for the patient is a core ingredient in the healing process of psychotherapy. I am not talking about romantic love or sexual love or sentimentality. I am referring to the wide spectrum of love: kindness, compassion, encouragement, warmth, nonjudgment, emotional feeding, hugs, gentle challenge and celebration of growth. Over the many years of my practice I have come to understand that techniques, theories and professionalism are all important, but insufficient for deeply effective therapy.

When I look back at my own training in traditional psychoanalysis and ask the question "How often was the idea of compassion or loving-kindness toward your patients mentioned?" or when I ask therapists trained in other theories of psychotherapy, "How often were you encouraged to love your clients?" the response is the same, "Rarely, if at all." What a profound dilemma that creates. Our natural inclination to be a caring human being is not even acknowledged as an important aspect of being a psychotherapist. How are we supposed to interpret that absence? Does it mean that compassion and other acts of love are unnecessary or, even worse, unprofessional or harmful? Early in this book I describe my struggles with this dilemma and how my work evolved into a more heart-centered approach.

What does it mean to have a more heart-centered approach? First of all, I am not implying that other ways of working are cold-hearted or that other therapists are uncaring. A heart-centered approach simply calls for a greater awareness that the therapist's love is a cardinal aspect of effective therapy. It means the therapist is more openly expressive of nonsexual, nonromantic, nonsentimental forms of love. This is especially true in offering consoling touch when appropriate, in working through what I call *love blocks* and in being a *sanctuary* for our patients. Second, there are certain therapeutic issues that cannot be resolved at the level of consciousness at which they exist. Cognitive, behavioral and analytic methods will be minimally effective. They are areas in which another aspect of consciousness—the realm of the heart—of both therapist and patient needs to be actively engaged. These issues include the patient's need to forgive themselves, most major life decisions and those emotional territories that are too overwhelming for the small heart of ordinary consciousness.

Each chapter in this book focuses, from a heart-centered perspective, on a particular aspect of psychotherapeutic work that I feel has been insufficiently addressed in training and supervision or has not been addressed at all. For example, at some point in therapy, every patient has something for which they need to forgive themselves. Perhaps they hurt someone they loved, or they have failed to do something needed. Perhaps they harbor an expectation of themselves that they are unable to fulfill. Generally we were not trained as clinicians in how to help people forgive themselves. It is as if the issue of forgiveness is considered to be in the realm of spirituality or religion and not an aspect of psychotherapeutic work. In the rare instance that self-forgiveness is mentioned as a therapeutic goal, no one talks about techniques. Most therapists develop some areas of special interest and expertise that emerge from our own histories. In my own life, overwhelmed with guilt after initiating a divorce, I was lost and despairing. From this experience, I have evolved a perspective and techniques to help patients to forgive themselves. In this book, the chapter on "Self-Forgiveness" begins with that personal journey.

One of the most important goals of a heart-centered approach to therapy, perhaps *the* most important, is to increase people's ability to give and receive love. My particular focus has been on the oftentimes pervasive, usually unconscious, psychological blocks that we all have to being receptive to love in the many forms that it is available to us. Almost twenty years ago, I coauthored a well received book entitled *Love Blocks, Breaking the Patterns That Undermine Relationships*. In *Working From the Heart*, I am revisiting that topic from the perspective of a more heart-centered approach, honed by years of additional practice.

How often we have difficulty in easily receiving compliments, being comfortable with physical affection, accepting help when it is offered or asking for help from people we know would assist us. It is difficult for many of us to accept and honor the myriad ways in which people show love that do not fit with the ways we want this love expressed. Why do we block opportunities for love in our lives? How can we lessen or remove these barriers? The answers to these questions are the focus of the "Love Blocks" chapter.

We know that gentle touch is one of the most ordinary acts of human kindness toward someone who is suffering. Yet, whether or not to touch patients is one of the most controversial questions in the practice of psychotherapy. Some therapists resolve this dilemma by making a therapeutic rule—*Thou shalt not touch*. From a heart-centered perspective, however, that dictum deprives patients of one of the most healing expressions of love and compassion for someone in pain—nonsexual, nonromantic, consoling touch. In the "Touch" chapter I encourage therapists to slog through the conflicts about touch in order to discern in what situations and for what patients gentle touch is the right therapeutic action.

From my perspective, in general our male patients need a heart-centered approach more than the women do. In the "Men" chapter I discuss three aspects of a more heart-centered therapeutic mode that are particularly effective with my male patients: educating them about the language of the heart; using self-disclosure to model having a deeper connection to their inner emotional landscape; employing traditional male metaphors such as the *warrior*, the *provider* and the *toolbox* as a bridge to their emotional lives.

At some point in their therapy most of our patients will be faced with some major decision that will change the direction of their life. The typical therapeutic approach to life crises in the current atmosphere of managed care is to emphasize a solution-focused perspective. From my experience, however, because the larger human dilemmas cannot be resolved at the level of consciousness at which they exist, that approach is rarely helpful. My heart-centered approach focuses on viewing the conflicting ideas and emotions the patient expresses as emanating from diverse parts of the personality. The role of therapist is to help the patient to develop compassion for all these parts, increase their tolerance for the tension among these often opposing inner voices, and get the various parts of the personality to work together for the good of the whole person. Following this model, I have developed a technique I call "The Council," in which, the Higher Self of the patient takes on the role of an inner "wise elder" who holds the questions, *What is in my best interest to resolve this issue? How can I honor all the parts of myself and create a synthesis of their ideas?*

During the process of therapy most patients become aware that they have internalized a feeling or perspective that really does not belong to them. "It" doesn't fit who they are now or connect to the actual circumstances of their current life. I call these pervasive intrapsychic intruders *implants*—thoughts, feelings or world-views that have been implanted in the personality by family (sometimes for many generations), class, ethnic group, religion or by the overall culture. Some examples of *implants* I've observed in my practice are: an anxiety about money that does not fit the patient's actual financial situation; a pervasive judgmental or critical attitude toward others; a fearfulness or sadness that does not seem to have roots in the patient's personal history; a general mistrust of others. In the "Uprooting the Implants" chapter, using metaphor and imagery, I teach patients to let go of these implants so that they may release what does not belong in their inner landscape.

Our *small hearts*, the emotional hearts of ordinary human consciousness, are profoundly limited in their ability to hold all that we need to hold in our roles as psychotherapists. We are exposed on a daily basis to a potentially numbing amount of suffering. We need to navigate the sometimes turbulent waters of transference and countertransference. We experience our own periodic fluctuations in energy and mood that make it difficult to be fully present. We are asked to be compassionate and loving toward patients we don't like. In the "Small Heart, Big Heart" chapter I describe ways of engaging an aspect of our Higher Self, our *big heart*, so that we can be a loving presence in all of these situations.

Because so many of our patients come from families or other relationships that were physically or psychologically unsafe, it is essential that we find ways to convey to them that we are offering ourselves to be a place of safety and refuge—a sanctuary. The core question for us to ask ourselves is, *How do I communicate to my patients verbally and nonverbally the message that they are entering a safe haven in which they will be received with warmth, kindness and dignity?* The "Sanctuary" chapter presents ways of answering that query both within the therapeutic relationship and in the atmosphere of our office space. Since some of the therapeutic work occurs between sessions it is also important to help our patients develop other ways of finding sanctuary in their everyday lives. Some examples that I discuss include: taking solitary walks in nature, creating a sacred space at home and doing regular journal writing.

A central issue that we all struggle with as therapists is taking care of ourselves. How can we sustain an optimal level of open-hearted presence when we are exposed to so much suffering? How do we do that hour after hour, day after day, for years and not become exhausted, overwhelmed, emotionally distant, resentful or numb? The draining nature of our work requires that we find reliable ways to recharge our physical and psychological batteries. We are very good at taking care of others, yet many of us are not good at taking care of ourselves. Why is that? The chapter on "Recharging" explores that question and describes ways of restoring ourselves both outside the therapeutic space and during sessions.

Our culture generally does not honor the role of elder. My thirty-five years of practice and my experience with cancer have propelled me to reflect at length upon the issues that I raise in *Working From the Heart*. As an elder in my field, I offer this writing as my legacy to the next generations of psychotherapists. I am profoundly grateful to those who have contributed to *my* formation as a therapist, upon whose shoulders I stand. I am also grateful that my heart-centered way of being a therapist is uniquely mine, evolving over time, a full expression of who I am. It is my hope that these essays will encourage other therapists to find their own unique synthesis of open-heartedness and professionalism, informed by theory and technique, that truly expresses who they are.

I have intentionally written this book in an informal, nonacademic style. It is not intended to be used as a textbook, therefore there are no footnotes or references. Instead, the image that has carried me through the writing of this book is of me and you, the readers, gathered around the woodstove in the living room of my home in the country on a chilly evening. We are a group of psychotherapists coming together from a wide spectrum of theories and perspectives about our healing work, with a range of years of experience. I am sharing my ideas gleaned from all the years of my practice. Let's have a conversation.

①

WISDOM OF THE HEART

As Maria told her story, the reasons for her "river of anxiety" became eminently clear. Her father was a compulsive gambler who would periodically disappear for a week or more. She never knew when or if he would return. During those times, her mother was depressed and highly anxious, often saying, "Maybe this time he won't come back." One thing that was predictable was that, when he did return, there would be a huge fight between her parents. Her father had a paranoid streak and often he would accuse her mother of having an affair while he was gone. Maria recalled a terrifying time when she was five years old and witnessed her father push her mother down a flight of stairs. Her mother, never meek or submissive in the face of her husband's abuse, always fought back regardless of the danger.

"One night," Maria remembered, "I woke up feeling afraid that something bad was going to happen. I went downstairs and saw my mother in the kitchen with a big knife in her hand. She was headed toward their bedroom. I started to scream, 'Please mommy, don't kill him!' She looked at me and then slowly put the knife away."

At that moment, I said softly to Maria, "My heart goes out to that little girl. How terrifying that was for her." Maria started to cry and so I got up and handed her a tissue. She began sobbing. Then I said, "I feel like you could use a hug, would it be okay with you if I gave one?" She opened her arms and I sat alongside her as she wept in my arms.

At our next session, Maria shared with me how comforted she felt by my words and acts of loving-kindness. During the week between our sessions, those frightening childhood memories had returned. As she remembered the soothing tone of my empathic response, me handing her a tissue and my warm hug, she felt consoled and loved. She could also feel the terror dissipating. During the process of her therapy, Maria would periodically tell me how that moment and others like it were the most helpful sessions. They made her feel that I really cared about her and that she was a loveable person.

Of course I know that other therapists have similar stories. We might share these anecdotes with each other and sometimes someone will even write about them, but it is rare. These simple moments of intimacy, when we step outside of our professional role, are vital expressions of compassionate love and human connection. We do this work because of a heartfelt desire to alleviate suffering. Yet the current emphasis on cognitive techniques and behavioral outcomes has caused us to suppress and undervalue the overt expression of this basic human love and compassion. In another time, we would have called this *agape*, the nonerotic love of one human being for another.

Techniques are important. Theories of personality and psychotherapy are important. Analysis and diagnosis are important. But all of these are insufficient in and of themselves. Kindness is also important. Compassion is important. The concern and caring we show our patients are essential parts of effective therapy. They are not extras; they are central. Yet increasing our capacity for empathy, developing a compassionate presence, and gaining a heartfelt understanding of why and how human love and kindness can help to heal us are either absent or barely touched on in our training as psychotherapists.

THE DILEMMA

In a culture that has romanticized, sexualized or sentimentalized love in the media images that explode around us day in and day out, it is difficult to talk about love without raising suspicions or being dismissed as "new age-y." But, really, it is a quality of being that I am talking about. I am not talking about romantic love, sexual love or simple sentimentality. These expressions of love would be unhelpful and even harmful for our patients. I am talking about the ability to embody a wider spectrum of love: kindness, compassion, encouragement, warmth, nonjudgment, cheerleading, hugs, gentle challenge, emotional nurturance, warm-heartedness, limit setting and celebration of growth. Most of the therapists I've known in my three decades of practice have been compassionate and caring people sincerely motivated to help. Yet if you ask them, "How often in your training was the idea of compassion or loving-kindness toward your patients mentioned?" or, "How often were you encouraged to love your clients?" most will say, "Rarely, if at all." Colleagues tell me that what was emphasized were theories, techniques and ways of maintaining professional objectivity and distance. The message inherent in this is that our natural inclination to care for patients is unhelpful, perhaps even harmful. Certainly it is unnecessary. What a powerful dilemma that creates! If I want to be a professional who helps people I must suppress the part of myself that is a loving human being.

The early giants of psychotherapy—Freud, Jung, Klein, Assagioli, and others—wanted their ideas to be accepted by the scientific and academic communities of their era. They needed venues in which to lecture and places to publish so that their theories of personality and techniques of treatment could be expressed. If they had emphasized that one of the most essential aspects of healing the wounded and suffering psyches of their patients was the therapist's compassionate heart, these early analysts would have been laughed at and exposed to professional humiliation. Many acknowledged their more tender-hearted feelings for their patients in letters to trusted friends, hoping to avoid the judgmental eyes of colleagues. Others simply assumed that the care and warmth they expressed for their patients wasn't that important to the treatment. Nevertheless, they did love their patients. Some, like Melanie Klein, who went on record with their divergent viewpoints on treatment approaches, were heavily criticized and publicly discredited. Sander Ferenczi was so marginalized that he experienced a nervous breakdown. The early analysts were part of the patriarchal subculture of the European scientific community in which the emphasis was on rational, clinical approaches that could be empirically validated. The notion that developing a caring relationship was essential in the treatment of patients would have been rebuked as irrational and unscientific. But these early therapists routinely formed friendships with patients. They loaned patients money or charged minimal fees. They invited them out to dinner or lunch and encouraged some to join their professional groups. And all of this went on while the patients remained in treatment. Today these ways of being with patients would be labeled as boundary violations and unprofessional. Some would consider them unethical.

While I am not advocating that we invite patients into our homes or loan them money, I am raising these questions—*How do we reconnect to the intentionality at the root of our work—to facilitate the healing of our patients' wounded psyches? How do we synthesize scientific knowledge and the fundamental qualities of human love? How do we do our work from a place of heart/mind—where heart and mind are not at odds with each other but act in unison?*

From my perspective, the choice between being professional and being open-hearted presents a false dichotomy. The resolution of the dilemma is simple—both are essential. Our challenge is to attain the correct balance. Certainly our patients benefit from our years of training and experience in theories, research and techniques. Without that we would be reinventing the wheel with each patient. On the other hand, the psychological research on successful therapeutic outcomes consistently shows that *our relationship with the patient is the core ingredient of the healing process.* Like the early therapists, most of us are more loving toward our patients than we probably admit. As we recognize that this loving attitude is an essential healing component of the therapeutic relationship, we can become less hesitant and more open in expressing that caring with our patients.

From a scientific perspective, recent brain imaging research supports the inherent value of a consistent and sustained loving presence. Using the language of "resonance," the thinking goes something like this: as infants, we develop a resonance with our parents that sets down neurochemical pathways in our brains. These pathways continue to be reinforced all through childhood. As we grow into adulthood we likely will be attracted to people and relationships that are "in tune" with those neurochemical pathways and, thus, similar to our relationships with our parents. What can change a negative (abusive, anxious, depressed) neurochemical pattern is consistent and sustained contact with someone or some others who resonate differently (kind, grounded, joyful). Being in the frequent presence of someone who expresses loving-kindness, compassion, and genuine human affection can, over time, "repave" those pathways in our brains in a way that brings them into attunement with these qualities.

From this vantage point, as therapists we can produce a shift in the neurochemical patterns of our patients by being more overtly compassionate and caring. We offer a relationship in which the patient can begin to internalize, *psychologically and physiologically,* the feeling that others can love them and that they deserve love. Initially they may block or misinterpret the loving and caring feelings; over time they can come to feel nourished by them. The push and pull between science and heart, behaviorism and humanism is an ongoing dilemma in our field that is skewed right now on the side of cognitive-behavioral approaches. There have always been voices raised in an effort to bring in more of the humanistic qualities of our work. At its core, my message as an elder in the field of psychotherapy is to embrace a more heart-centered approach to our work.

COMING OUT OF HIDING

At the beginning of my work as a psychotherapist over thirty-five years ago, I realized that I needed more training. I was accepted at a well-known post-doctoral institute for psychoanalysis in New York. Although quite eclectic in their approaches, most of the faculties' lineage was Freudian. In that tradition the analyst serves as a "blank screen." The patient reclines on the couch while the analyst sits behind him, leaving the patient unable to see any facial expressions and only experiencing the analyst's nonverbal communication through vocal intonation, or the sounds of the analyst's shifting body positions. Since he reveals nothing of himself, whatever perceptions the patient has of the analyst are considered to be projections of his early childhood experiences with parents. For example, if the patient's father was critical, the patient would experience the analyst as critical and react to him from that perspective. In that

Freudian tradition it is the "working through" of that transference that is the central healing dynamic of the therapy. While this description is an over-simplification of the Freudian model, it does depict a central tenet of that training, which is that it is essential that the therapist not reveal who he is because that would interfere with the development and working through of the transference.

Initially the classical Freudian approach suited my own needs. We've all had the experience as clinicians of hiding behind the therapist's chair to avoid facing our own problems. In my case, it was as if my sensitive heart was in an inner cave afraid to come out, waiting for some clue that it was safe. Much of my childhood and adolescence were spent trying to survive emotionally and physically in a home colored by my father's psychological abuse. Though my father was capable of expressing kindness and caring, my earliest imprint of him was of his tyrannical presence. He had little tolerance for his emotionally sensitive son. My mother was a gentle soul who counterbalanced my father by trying to maintain peace in the house at any cost. She would often forewarn us not to upset my father. And though, thankfully, she was a gentle presence, her river of inner fearfulness inhibited expressions of warmth and physical affection. Outside my home, in the crucible of the playground of the working class housing project where we lived, I kept my feelings hidden from view.

Later on, as I began my training to be a psychotherapist, I quickly realized that I needed to begin my own therapy. I am profoundly grateful to my first therapist. He was a helpful presence during a very dark time of depression and self-hatred. The atmosphere of his warm, wood-paneled office was comforting. His salient questions, asked without judgment, were ones I had to begin to consider: *How had the experience of my father's drinking contributed to the level of anxiety that I felt? How had my father's criticism influenced my sense of self-hatred?* His insights and the gentleness of his approach helped to lift the despair and lessen my anxiety. He helped me to see myself as a sensitive, warm-hearted person by nature, and to like those qualities in myself. Yet he was a traditionally trained psychoanalyst who sat behind me while I lay on the couch. He never disclosed anything about himself, nor were there any warm physical exchanges between us. His subtle smile before and after our sessions suggested that he cared about me, but left me wondering, *Does he really care about me or is he just doing his job?* This absence of any overt expression of affection mimicked my father's emotional distance, the ways he kept his feelings hidden and his life stories untold. I never questioned his approach; I simply accepted that this was what therapists did.

Like most beginning therapists, at first I emulated what my therapist did. Yet, over time, I saw what was missing for me in his approach. I would have liked him to share more of his personal story. It would have helped me to know that he, too, had been through some dark periods. It would have provided a beacon of hope. And, while I *sensed* his empathy, if he had expressed it more directly and more often, I would have felt more deeply cared for.

My second experience in therapy was with the director of the psychoanalytic institute where I was studying. The first few months of my analysis were spent interpreting my refusal to lie on the couch as I had in my first therapy. Against tradition, I insisted on face-to-face interaction. Eventually, my therapist relented and we sat in chairs facing each other. After one very painful, tear-filled session, I stood up and asked him for a hug. He embraced me warmly. I knew that he was taking a risk in doing this. That he stepped out of his traditional psychoanalytic role to be simply a loving human being with me is something that still fills my heart with gratitude. His hug was genuine and let me know that he was a warm-hearted person. When we talked at our next session and I asked him why he had not initiated the hug and why it didn't happen more often, he simply said that therapists are not supposed to touch their patients. I felt sad that this therapeutic rule meant I was deprived of his warmth and that he was unable to feel free to be an authentic loving person.

During this time of psychological healing, I was also exploring different paradigms of thought that broadened my understanding of the human psyche. I devoured the works of Carl Jung, Carl Rogers, Rollo May and other psychologists as well as a variety of Buddhist and Taoist spiritual readings. At the age of forty, I began a Zen meditative practice. This gave me a vehicle for developing my spiritual life and a tool to reduce my anxiety. When I became aware of how much the meditation practice was helping me, I started to teach the breathing techniques to my patients. Hesitantly at first, and not naming the work as meditation, I began teaching a kind of breathing similar to Herbert Benson's "relaxation response," although when I initiated this work with patients I was unaware of his research. I would say to my patients, "This breathing technique has been helpful in my life, perhaps it will help you too." They responded positively and were grateful to have a tool that helped to reduce their own anxiety.

At this point, a younger therapist might ask, "What's the big deal about teaching relaxation breathing?" but twenty-five years ago, for a psychoanalytically trained and oriented psychotherapist, it was an unusual and important step, part of my evolution toward a model of treatment based on greater self-disclosure and reciprocity with my patients.

Many of my early patients also came from alcoholic backgrounds like I did, and from families where they experienced a lot of emotional deprivation. Over time, I discovered that the psychoanalytic model did not work for me in treating them. Insights into the reasons for their psychological patterns helped, but were not enough. I realized that my patients needed more from me. As patients do, they became great teachers for me.

I could see how positively it affected them when I said a simple "Welcome" or "I'm glad to see you" at the beginning of a session. This was especially true for patients who felt unwanted from birth, or like they'd been a burden to their parents. My patients felt nurtured by the coffee or tea offered in my waiting room. Most would bring a cup in and sip it during our sessions. They welcomed the contact of my warm handshake before or after sessions. When, in response to their stories about the difficulties of growing up in an alcoholic home, I shared that my father was also an alcoholic, they were grateful for the empathic connection. I, too, had lived in that environment and recovered. Their sense of hope increased. People appreciated when I took extra care to acknowledge and celebrate their moments of personal growth. Or they often cried when I said "My heart goes out to you for your pain." After a particularly difficult session, some patients would open their arms to be hugged when I asked, "I feel like you need a hug, would it be okay with you if I gave you one?"

When placed in the context of the emotional unavailability of an alcoholic parent and the often emotionally depleted state of the other parent, my patients' responses were easy to understand. Patients with other kinds of traumatic histories were also emotionally hungry for the open-hearted caring of a surrogate parent. They appreciated my genuineness and warmth, saying that it felt like an invitation to be more open with me. For these patients, the professionally distant, non-revealing therapeutic stance and cognitive approach of the psychoanalytic method was too reminiscent of their depriving and often emotionally unavailable parents. They responded to my new approach as a very different kind of relationship that was helping to undo the effects of inadequate parenting. Of course some patients experienced transferential reactions to my expressions of love, but as we worked through these responses, they would often tell me that I made them feel safe and cared for.

A few years into using this heart-centered approach to my work, I took a big professional risk. I submitted an article on my way of working with adult children of alcoholics to a prestigious psychoanalytical journal and it was published! I had finally come out of the closet with my non-traditional approach. This way of working that was more genuine to my essential nature could be an effective alternative to the current conventional practice. After the article was published, I felt greater freedom to be open about this aspect of my work.

RISKS

Of course this heart-centered approach to psychotherapy has its risks for both therapist and patient. For the therapist, being both a professional with expertise and a warm, open-hearted human being makes us feel vulnerable. How we deal with these feelings will depend on how others have treated our open hearts throughout our lives and how our emotional needs are being met in our current life. As my own story shows, my father's need to be the dominant force in our home coupled with my mother striving for "peace at any cost" did not create an atmosphere that encouraged free expression of feelings. Outside my home, the playground was a psychological war zone. Verbal humiliation, competitive anger and periodic fights were the norm. My mettle was tested there every day. It was not a wise place to expose my emotional vulnerability. When I married in my mid-twenties, my wife carried her own wounds from childhood. We both struggled with limited skills in expressing verbal and physical affection. It was not a good combination for a lasting, happy marriage.

Reflecting on my early years as a therapist it is clear to me that, because of this background, my heart was not yet open. While I am sure that I was a help to my patients, I was still in a self-protective place. Maintaining a professional distance and being a psychoanalytic "blank screen" suited me just fine. As I worked through emotional issues in my own psychotherapy, a shift gradually occurred in my work as a therapist. My heart opened more. I realized that I often had been unconsciously reliving a part of my childhood—closing up in anticipation of how a patient would feel coming in to an appointment in much the same way I had self-protectively prepared myself for my father's entrance into our home. Now I whole-heartedly feel a sense of welcome as patients enter my office. As a young clinician, I was also particularly conflicted about being open-hearted with female patients, fearing that I might unconsciously try to get from them the affection that my mother and wife were both unable to give me. Now that my own emotional needs are fulfilled, I am freer in being warm-hearted with the women I work with.

These counter-transferential issues blocked me in my early years as a therapist from being more present and genuine in my work. It is important for each of us as therapists to go through our own personal therapy process. It will help to prevent us from being shut down because of our projections that patients will hurt us like others have in the past.

Doing our own psychological work is the foundation of protecting our patients from our own un-worked-out childhood issues. It will prevent us from using them to fulfill our unmet yearnings. To further protect and care for our patients, it is essential for us to consider how any particular expression of love will impact upon a particular person. How will she or he respond to a warm greeting, praise, a hug, a celebratory "high five" or other overt expression of love? How we show love will depend on our knowledge of the wounds they carry. How have they been hurt? How open or closed are they to emotional closeness? What is their degree of emotional hunger? Do they feel worthy of being loved? These are complex, often murky waters that are challenging to navigate. We need to take sufficient time to understand a central question—*what are the wounds that block our patients' receptivity to love?* From my way of thinking about it, each of our patients has one or more patterns, usually unconscious, that block them from receiving the love that is available to them from us and others in their lives. In a later chapter I will discuss the roots of some of these "love blocks" and how we can work with them from a heart-centered perspective within the therapeutic relationship.

Throughout this book I will be advocating for us as therapists to bring our hearts more into our relationships with our patients. However, I am not saying that all they need is our love. We are not just kind, loving friends. We are professionals with a broad base of theoretical knowledge and skills coupled with years of experience. What I am encouraging is a return to our original intentions in entering into this life work. Most of us had a heartfelt desire to help others, to lessen their pain and suffering. By reconnecting to that initial intention and by expanding our awareness of the myriad ways in which our hearts can facilitate healing, then our patients benefit from a synthesis of our minds and our hearts.

②

SELF-FORGIVENESS

Throughout my years as a psychologist it has often been my own life experiences that have taught and prepared me to know how to help my patients. I learned about self-forgiveness eighteen years ago when I told my wife of twenty-four years and my two sons that I had fallen in love with someone else and would be leaving them. They had no warning, no preparation. The amount of pain I caused was beyond anything that I had ever imagined. I will always remember witnessing my younger son writhing in pain on the floor curled up in the fetal position, his brother standing in disbelief, tears cascading down his face, and the waves and waves of pain, sadness and anger of their mother. I caused the greatest pain of their lives to the people I loved the most.

At that time most of my identity was framed around myself as the protector of my family and the healer of the pain of others. Yet now I was the cause of so much pain. For a long time, I was unable to reconcile the image I carried of who I was and the intense guilt I felt for the pain I had caused. I thought often of killing myself. I would imagine jumping in front of a moving car as I walked along the road. What stopped me was the thought of what that would do to my sons, my beloved Jeanne and the driver of the car. To me it would bring relief; to them it would bring more pain. I had already caused enough pain. What could I do to move through this most excruciating emotional state?

I knew I needed forgiveness. I knew, too, that it wouldn't come from my ex-wife, or my sons, at least not anytime soon. I knew how to forgive others, but not how to forgive myself. Nothing in my training as a psychologist or in my spiritual training was helpful. I was totally lost. So in desperation I started pleading to God, to the ones I hurt, to whoever might be listening. In private moments on my daily walks in the woods, I would say, *Please forgive me. Please help me to forgive myself. Please help me. Help!!* over and over. Gradually images would spontaneously float into my mind. Sometimes they were of Jesus and his sacred heart, or of Buddha smiling gently. Sometimes I would have images of being carried and held by a loving father, or of sitting by a brook or standing under a waterfall and being cleansed by the cascades of water washing over me. I had images of sitting by the beach and listening to the rhythm of the waves, of standing amidst a warm and enveloping mist. I spent time in the woods almost every day for months. On these walks I would often fall, sobbing, on the ground in a small grove of giant old pines. Or I would simply sit on the ground with my back up against a tree—I rested there and felt cared for. There were two trees in particular which, over time, I came to think of as my "mother" and "father" trees. I would sit beneath them and plead for help. The images of Jesus or Buddha or forgiving parents would come to me. Gradually the suicidal thoughts left. My heavy emotional weight began to lift and a place inside me began to open. I felt lighter. The darkness that had filled my heart for so long was being transformed into light. Little by little, I simply had a sense that I was forgiven. I could not say at the time exactly where it came from, but the process taught me a lot about self-forgiveness.

SELF-FORGIVENESS IS NOT A RATIONAL PROCESS

From my experience, I have come to articulate four important aspects of the self-forgiveness process. First and foremost, while there are certain steps we can take to facilitate the work, self-forgiveness unfolds according to its own timetable. The other three aspects have to do with using petitionary prayer, the healing power of nature, and the importance of using some kind of guided imagery as a way of tapping into other realms of consciousness.

Most of us know the experience of forgiveness by way of forgiving another or feeling forgiven by another. We know it by its effects on others or ourselves. We know the feeling of warm-heartedness and lightness of being that comes with forgiving another, or the feeling of serenity that comes when the weight of guilt lifts because we feel forgiven by another. We know that it usually happens over time. While the qualities of self-forgiveness are the same—lightness of being, serenity, taking time—the source is somewhat different.

I experience forgiveness as existing both inside of us and outside of us. Within us I call the source of forgiveness our personal higher consciousness—our Deep Self, Higher Self, or Soul. The outside source I call God, the Divine, Higher Power or the Source.

Oftentimes patients are surprised when I mention the notion of self-forgiveness and they ask, "Why do I need to forgive myself?" For some the answer is because the person they have wounded is unable to forgive them. They may never be able to forgive or it might be many years before they can forgive. For some of my patients, the other person is dead and the possibility of being forgiven or making amends to them is gone. For some people it would be detrimental to their ongoing relationship to ask the other person for forgiveness at this time.

In some cases the other person *has* forgiven them or they *have* made amends, yet they still feel guilty. It feels as though the forgiveness from the outside source was helpful, but not sufficient. Some religious people feel that God has forgiven them, but they still feel guilty. They say, "I feel that God has forgiven me and I know that should be enough but I still feel guilty. I guess my faith is just not strong enough." They feel a mixture of hopelessness and inadequacy because the faith that they have relied upon is not sufficiently helpful. Oftentimes this also adds to their guilt—"If only my faith was strong enough . . ."

For some of my patients their own self-expectations are the source of their guilt. If they've failed to live up to some inner expectation, who else can forgive them but themselves? For many other patients, the source of their guilt is unconscious and needs to be unearthed and dealt with by the Higher Self.

Self-forgiveness is not a rational process. It cannot be attained through reasoning, linear thinking, intellectual understanding, or any other ego processes. Perhaps that is why it is not discussed in psychotherapy training. Professional training, for the most part, focuses on cognitive processes. However, because forgiveness happens in the territory of the heart and spirit, it can only be attained in those realms. As therapists, we need to find ways of tapping into those other realms of consciousness that transcend our everyday ego processes. The task of psychotherapy is to create an opening so that the forgiveness that is available to us can enter from both inside and outside, from the Deep Self and the Divine. Much of the psychotherapeutic work is preparatory; it is about removing personal blocks of unworthiness to feeling forgiven, and about helping the patient stay with a difficult process. While it is often part of our religious, ethnic, familial or cultural teachings that certain things are unforgiveable, our work is to examine the sources of these beliefs and help our patients to let them go. From my experience with these realms of higher consciousness, the ordinarily incomprehensible is true—everything and everyone is forgiveable.

PRAYER AS A PLEA FOR HELP

One of the first steps in the process of self-forgiveness is a particular kind of prayer, a personal plea for help from something or someone larger than oneself. I explain to patients that these prayers are a way of tapping into the realms of heart and spirit that are beyond our ordinary, everyday experience of consciousness. Sometimes these prayers are a kind of petition that is reaching out to an external source of forgiveness—God, Buddha, the Tao, the Source. What patients call this depends on their particular spiritual path. These prayers also attempt to connect us to some internal source of forgiveness. I tell my patients that they are calling on some aspect of their personal consciousness that transcends their everyday mind, a source of inner wisdom that knows what is best for them. I use the terms Higher Self, Deep Self or Soul to give a name to that source of inner wisdom. When one of those terms doesn't resonate for someone, we find something that does.

In this initial stage of self-forgiveness work it is common for patients to go into a state of "forgetting." They often forget what we talked about in the last session and, unless it's written down, they almost always forget about the prayers we talked about. This is quite understandable given the difficult nature of this work and the power that self-sabotaging parts of the personality can have in the unconscious. To guard against this desire to forget, I always give my patients index cards with prayers written on them. These are some that I most often suggest:

Please forgive me
Help me to forgive myself
Help me to feel forgiven
Help me to forgive myself for not being perfect

I ask my patients to say the prayer that feels most resonant in their heart and suggest that they reword it if need be in a way that feels right to them. I recommend they put it in their wallet or purse, in a shirt pocket next to their heart, in their car or in some other place where they will see it often. I also suggest taking the prayer with them to some special place in nature. Contemplating the words while walking in the woods, by the ocean, along a brook or up to the top of a hill deepens the efficacy of the prayer. I also explain to my patients that in many ancient spiritual traditions it was common for people, whenever they needed some deep psychospiritual healing, to go away from the distractions of ordinary life and go into the natural world. This form of retreat into some place in nature fostered greater access to other, nonrational, realms of consciousness both within and outside of themselves. People from these ancient cultures viewed these nature settings as sacred places in which deep healing occurred.

RALPH

Ralph, a tall, lanky, Vietnam vet, still struggles thirty-five years later with the guilt of what he did during the war. The media images and stories about the Iraq war have again triggered memories and anxiety attacks.

A year into our work together, he was still unable to talk about the killings and other horrors he witnessed and in which he took part. He has made efforts to make amends by traveling to Vietnam to do service work and by financially supporting several Vietnamese families. These actions have been helpful, but insufficient. He still feels weighed down by the guilt and knows that it blocks his ability to fully enjoy his life.

When I talked with Ralph about the need for self-forgiveness, I gave him an index card that said *Help me to feel forgiven.* I asked him to close his eyes, say the mantra (he preferred that word to prayer), breathe deeply into his belly, and exhale through his mouth, imagining that some of the guilt was being released. After fifteen minutes of saying this mantra quietly to himself while doing this intentional breathing, he opened his eyes. "I feel lighter," he said. "Thirty-five years ago, as soon as we were discharged, someone should have taught us this." Ralph started to become tearful, sighed deeply, and then in a strong, firm tone said, "You should be doing this with the guys returning from Iraq. I don't want them to go through years of what I've been through. This is what they should be doing in the VA now." I nodded my head, felt warmth in my heart and said, "Yes, and now you and I can begin this long process of self-forgiveness."

I encouraged Ralph to repeat the mantra *Help me to feel forgiven* in private moments between sessions. In addition to the index card, he wrote the phrase in a journal that he brought to our sessions. Periodically, in subsequent sessions, I would ask, "Are you saying that mantra?" Embarrassed, he would report that he'd done it only a few times. With a warm smile I would reply, "Of course, that's what happens to most people; that's how guilt works. It tries to undermine the process by getting you to *not* do something that would be helpful in healing the guilt." He grinned and, with my continued encouragement, gradually repeated the mantra more often between sessions.

Ralph loves to walk in the woods. It is a place of sanctuary from the travails of his everyday life. He also has a special fondness for trees—he particularly feels at home amidst the large, older ones. Whenever he talks about trees and how he loves to climb them, his whole being lights up. I nod my head, acknowledging our mutual connection to trees and thinking that he and I are members of the same branch of the human tribe.

The woods are also periodically a place of danger for Ralph. At unexpected moments, certain sounds and flashes of light can trigger memories of the war and he falls to the ground in a panic. At these moments he is back on patrol in the jungles of Vietnam surrounded by sniper fire. As his body remembers and Ralph hits the ground, he quickly looks around and replays an image of two of his buddies, dead, and hears the sounds of others who are wounded and moaning. As his therapist, I know that his walks in the woods can be a central part of his healing process and that Ralph needs to feel safe there. I suggest that whenever these memories come up he seek out some large guardian trees under which he can feel protected, do the deep breathing and repeat his self-forgiveness mantra.

Using Guided Imagery

After several weeks of saying his mantra, Ralph and I did our first imagery session. With his eyes closed, I instructed him to do the deep breathing for a few minutes and then asked him to imagine himself taking a walk in the woods. "These are safe woods to walk in, no harm can come to you here. Just imagine the sights, sounds and smells of the woods. After a while you will come to a clearing in the woods, a large open area surrounded by trees. In the middle of the clearing is a very large old tree rooted deeply in the earth. Stand by that tree and feel what it is like to be in the presence of this ancient tree. After a while invite some image of forgiveness to come out of the woods and approach you. Trust whatever image of forgiveness shows up at this moment. Just observe the image. Be in its presence and be open to how it is trying to help you feel forgiven."

The first few times we did this, the image that showed up for him was Ralph's wife. He particularly focused on her face with her warm, benevolent smile and her trusting, innocent eyes. In almost a whisper he said, "In the image it feels like her eyes are looking deeply into my soul. Even though she doesn't say a word, there is something about the way she is looking that is hard to describe. My heart feels warm and like a weight has been lifted off of me."

When I first started to do this forgiveness imagery, I would attempt to get the patient to analyze why a particular image was the image of forgiveness. At this point in my work, unless the patient spontaneously offers an explanation, I leave it alone, respecting that a powerful heart process is unfolding. Any intellectual analysis could intrude into the feelings and energy field of the heart work that is occurring. On several occasions working with Ralph, no specific image of forgiveness emerged from the woods. Instead he climbed up into the tree and felt cradled in its large limbs. Ralph revealed, "It feels like I am being comforted by a parent. My parents were never consoling to me. I wish I had experienced a parent like this tree." In those moments he was in the arms of a forgiving parent.

As his therapy unfolded Ralph talked more about his deep fondness and spiritual connection to trees. He earned his living through tree work: removing fallen trees, trimming limbs, giving guidance about what to do with diseased trees—Ralph was the person to call. People knew that he would do the work in a way that was respectful of the trees. As his love for trees increased, so concurrently did his sadness and guilt for the desecration of the natural world that he had contributed to as a soldier in Vietnam.

In contrast to what he had learned through his military training, Ralph continued to develop a deep relationship with the natural world. He felt an affinity for Native American traditions and resonated with their ideas about respect for the other creatures in nature and the notion of "warrior" as a protector, in contrast to our military idea of a warrior as a killer. As our work evolved, Ralph began to connect with what we called the *Heart Warrior* part of himself and called on this aspect of his personality to deal with the panic attacks and nightmares that were part of the traumatic residue of being in Vietnam.

During one of our imagery sessions, the Heart Warrior came to Ralph in the visage of a Native American elder with whom he had done some weekend workshops. In this imagery, the elder simply looked at Ralph with an expression of deep compassion. No words were spoken, but in his kind and loving presence, Ralph felt his burden of sadness and guilt ease. Afterwards, Ralph recalled a story about seeing this elder standing in a brook, weeping. When someone asked him why he was crying, the elder said simply, "The brook and I are one." For Ralph, this story reflected the elder's deep and compassionate connection to the natural world. He felt that the elder, as the image of his Heart Warrior, was conveying to him in a non-verbal way, nature's acceptance of Ralph's acts of atonement for his participation in the destruction that occurred during the war.

Although months would go by when we did not talk about Vietnam, Ralph's conversation eventually drifted back to the war. During one of these sessions, I asked him if there was something else about his experience in Vietnam for which he felt he needed forgiveness. After a long silence he replied, "Just being there." He hesitated before continuing, "I never allowed myself to think about it until now, but I feel like I took the easy way out. Other guys disagreed with the war and went to Canada and didn't come home for many years." Ralph started to shift around in the chair and put his head down, unable to look me in the eyes. Unwittingly he had opened a door into a territory of unconscious shame. He went on, "Some guys, when they were over there, realized what we were really doing and refused to fight anymore. They were court-martialed and sent to prison. They stood up for what they believed in and took the consequences. I did not. I took the easy way out. I smoked a lot of dope. I partied so I wouldn't have to be aware of what I really felt." These feelings of shame about being a coward, of not living up to his expectations of what a man should do, were an underneath layer of his guilt. At that moment, I felt tearful for this good man carrying the weight of cowardice. I was also grateful there was time left in the session to do some forgiveness imagery. This time, Ralph returned to climb into the arms of his ancient tree and soon felt a quiet acceptance and a sense of parental consolation. He felt again a lightening of his burden and a sense of knowing that he had stripped away another deep layer of guilt.

MICHELLE

Michelle, an auburn-haired woman in her mid-forties with chronic fatigue syndrome, walked slowly into my office for our first session and, in a weary tone, started to tell her story. "I used to be such an optimistic person, but this damn disease is wearing me down. It started eight years ago and I'm now in the middle of my sixth round of chronic fatigue. Each episode lasts for months and then, eventually, I return to normal. Each time I hope it's the last and then—Smack!—it hits again. I need

help coping with it better." Michelle reported that in the early stages of
the illness her husband had been very supportive, but during the third
recurrence he began to have regular angry outbursts. One night, Michelle groggily awakened in the middle of the night to see her husband
hovering over their bed just watching her. She recalled him saying, in a
very ominous tone, "I could kill you right now." Fearing for her safety
and knowing that her husband had crossed over a line and could no
longer tolerate her illness, she started the divorce process. That was two
years ago.

On Saturday mornings, when it is time for her ex-husband to pick up
the children for his weekend visitation, he is still very angry and refuses
to talk with Michelle. Although she has apologized many times to him,
e-mailing him numerous times to say, "I'm sorry," and has tried often
to have a dialogue, his response has been either anger or silence. She
wants to feel forgiven by him, yet she is beginning to wonder if that will
ever happen.

Our therapeutic journey has been focused on the psychological impact of the chronic fatigue on Michelle's sense of self, all the losses that
she has incurred because of her illness, and what psychological processes might be adding to and interacting with the physiological aspects
of her illness. We became increasingly aware that her guilt about initiating the divorce and breaking up the family was weighing her down and
contributing to the tiredness she experienced. Michelle said wistfully, "I
don't feel like myself, I am used to being resilient. The word my friends
used to use to describe me is 'spunky.' I feel like I've lost all my spunk.
Maybe the guilt about the divorce and the chronic fatigue are combin-
ing to break me down."

As often happens with chronic illness, the effects of it had worn down
the psychological resources of Michelle and her husband. This produced a deep emotional separation. Until Michelle became ill, she and
her husband had been good at resolving conflict. Prior to our sessions
she felt it was only her chronic fatigue that was producing his rage. But
as Michelle talked about their relationship, it became clear that her husband was reacting to other, less conscious, things as well. His childhood
history of caring for a retarded younger brother and sick father had also
contributed to his angry eruptions.

At this juncture in Michelle's story, it is important to point out one of the salient aspects of understanding how we can help people to heal guilt. Guilt often does not make rational sense. My telling her that she had good reason—her husband's escalating rage and the multiple reasons for it—to end the marriage, was not sufficient to lift Michelle's guilt. Cognitive insight did not help her to forgive herself. Deep healing eventually occurred only through other realms of consciousness—the realms of the heart and spirit.

Ever the optimist, she still held out hope that her ex-husband would forgive her. One day I said to Michelle, "Who knows if your husband will ever be able to forgive you. Even if he does, it will be helpful, but insufficient. You still need to forgive yourself for causing him pain and breaking up your family. Getting him to forgive you is not within your power. Forgiving yourself is." I gave her a card that said *Help me to forgive myself*, and told her to say it aloud as often as possible over several weeks.

For most of her life Michelle had loved to take solitary walks along the beach. She could be alone with her thoughts, away from household tasks and the demands of motherhood. She always returned home restored. Since the divorce, she had stopped taking these sojourns, saying that she could not find the time and was always so tired. This is one of the insidious ways guilt works—it blocks us from engaging in the activities that nourish and sustain us. I encouraged Michelle to resume these walks on the weekends that her kids were with their father. Water, I told her, is ubiquitous in forgiveness rituals and is a symbol of cleansing the soul and heart. My encouraging Michelle to take beach walks was intended to activate this archetypal symbolism that is part of the collective unconscious. In the meantime, we began some imagery sessions. With her eyes closed, I would have Michelle focus on her breathing as a way of entering into another state of consciousness. Then I would ask her to imagine walking alone on the beach, listening to the sounds of the waves, focusing on their ebbing and flowing. When I would feel that her breathing was deep and relaxed, I would say, "After a while stop and sit down, looking out toward the waves. While you are seated, some image of forgiveness will come toward you from a distance that feels comfortable to you. Just notice the image and how it feels to be in its presence. Be open to whatever happens." The first time we did this, what immediately came to Michelle was an image of Kuan Yin, the Chinese Buddhist goddess of compassion. In the imagery, Kuan Yin walked over to Michelle and sat alongside her looking out toward the waves. Sitting with her eyes closed, Michelle reported that she felt unburdened in the presence of this being. In subsequent sessions, I encouraged Michelle to dialogue with Kuan Yin. In these inner dialogues, she told Kuan Yin about the pain she had caused her husband and children by initiating the divorce. Kuan Yin remained simply a loving, nonjudgmental presence and Michelle would describe how she felt Kuan Yin's compassionate, forgiving energy flowing inside of her. It was heartwarming for me to witness her walk out of these sessions feeling lighter and lighter. In a later session, Michelle imagined Kuan Yin walking to the ocean's edge, cupping some water in her hands and pouring it over her body, starting at her feet. Michelle sobbed and sobbed as she experienced this inner ritual of self-forgiveness.

Michelle comes from a Christian religious background, but recently had found herself exploring some Eastern spiritual traditions and was particularly drawn to images of Kuan Yin. I told her that Kuan Yin's name translates as *the one who is there for those who weep,* and that it is common in the East to see shrines and statues of her by moving water. In some mysterious way, Michelle had tapped into this ancient spiritual figure, an archetypal image of feminine compassion and forgiveness, as a vehicle for her own healing. From my way of thinking about it, Kuan Yin also represented an aspect of Michelle's own consciousness—the deeply compassionate and forgiving facet of her Higher Self.

With most patients, self-forgiveness work is multilayered and occurs in cycles interspersed with sessions focused on other aspects of their lives. Toward the end of her therapy it became clear that for Michelle the guilt of leaving her husband tapped into a long forgotten memory of her mother's death. Her mother was an alcoholic who was prone to periodic bouts of depression. During her alcoholic ramblings she would often complain, "My children don't love me." As a child and young adult, Michelle felt the burden of grief that she could never be a good enough daughter who could make her mother feel loved. At twenty, when her mother died, she felt relieved and liberated. She would no longer have to worry about her mother's drinking; she was finally free to live her own life. It came as a shock when her father, who had been a target of his wife's verbal abuse, was devastated by her death. Michelle thought, "Why isn't he relieved like I am? He should be glad the abuse is over." When she saw how sad her other siblings and relatives were, Michelle felt quite guilty. "Perhaps my mother was right, I didn't love her enough." Michelle had never worked through her guilt about her mother and it had become deeply buried. Doing the forgiveness work about her divorce led to the uncovering of this forgotten episode. Again, I encouraged Michelle to return to her waterside walks and to imagine Kuan Yin accompanying her. After several weeks of taking her walks on the beach, Michelle came to her session and reported, "I've finally been able to forgive myself. Walking along the beach, imagining Kuan Yin with me, I felt forgiven. I don't feel guilty anymore about how relieved I was when my mother died. I know now that I loved her as best I knew how."

Archetypal Imagery

In doing this self-forgiveness work with Ralph and Michelle, I have intentionally used evocative archetypal images. The old, solid tree symbolizes the Higher Self, grounded and deeply rooted. It is associated with the ancient symbol of the Tree of Life that is an essential image in transformational healing in many cultures. The circular clearing in the woods is a metaphor for what Carl Jung would call a *temenos* place, an intrapsychic space where our Higher Self resides and where deep inner work is accomplished. In Michelle's therapy we used an image of a water place, evoking the archetypal image of spiritual cleansing. In Hindu, Christian, Muslim and other traditions, immersion in natural bodies of water and having sacred water poured over oneself are core elements of forgiveness rituals.

There are many symbols of forgiveness that we can tap into from these other realms of consciousness, any one or several of which may show up over time. As I have described my own self-forgiveness work, I would sometimes imagine traditional spiritual figures like Jesus, Buddha or Kuan Yin. At other times I would respond more to nature images, mainly water places, such as a waterfall, the ocean or a brook. Some patients relate more easily to an image from their own personal story such as a relative or friend who has shown them kindness or compassion.

Sometimes patients have had spontaneous images of animals, often a dog or other pet who has been a loving companion. Other creatures that have shown up in my patients' imagery are deer, butterflies, doves or other birds and even snakes. Oftentimes these patients have no personal associations to these particular animals; their frequency suggests that they emerge from the collective unconscious. These images symbolize different things to different people. All of them help to create an inner space for self-forgiveness to enter.

Some of my patients have had more abstract imagery experiences when I have asked them to imagine a forgiving presence. Rather than a visual image, they have experienced a feeling of warmth or light. Some feel a kind of energy or a sense of being enveloped in a gentle fog. Even if it doesn't make sense to the patient or to me as the therapist, there is good reason why a particular image shows up at a particular time. Sometimes the patient will have an understanding of why that particular image came to them, other times it remains a mystery. As therapists, we need to let go of our own need to understand why the image is occurring and simply work with what shows up, trusting that there are other, non-rational, forces at work. We are merely catalysts and holders of the psycho-spiritual space in which forgiveness can begin to happen.

Nature

From my experience, much of the healing in self-forgiveness work occurs outside the therapy room. Our patients need to go alone somewhere where they will feel safe and not self-conscious about what happens. Oftentimes in this work something unexpected occurs. They may suddenly start sobbing or fall to their knees or start talking out loud or chanting. Our patients need to feel free to allow their process to unfold from moment to moment. That is almost impossible if there are other people around; the presence of even a very supportive person can be quite inhibiting. Solitary time spent in a nature place that has unique significance for our patients creates a greater opening for self-forgiveness to occur more freely.

In many traditions, when deep inner work needs to be done, people have gone on solitary journeys into the natural world, away from the distractions and intimate connections of their ordinary life. It may be in the woods or at the water, in the desert or atop a mountain—the place becomes a safe container for the emerging emotions and a catalyst to connect to higher levels of consciousness both within and outside of ourselves. It is valuable to return to a particular place over time that has some special resonance for us. Some people know intuitively where to go. Others will experiment with a few places. If they trust deeply, at some point they will feel drawn to or beckoned by a place. After a while the place becomes imbued with the sacredness of our self-forgiveness work. Even as we walk toward this place we begin to feel a quieting down, an initial sense of peacefulness. Our Higher Self knows why we are here, that this is the right place for the healing that needs to occur. For this period of time this spot has become a sanctuary, a place of refuge and sacredness.

TONY

Tony was one of those people for whom the old-fashioned phrase, "he wears his heart on his sleeve" fit perfectly. Whenever Tony described his feelings, some part of his body would be moving. He would move forward in his chair, gesture with his hands, touch his heart. His feelings were so large and so "out there" that his body could not contain them. And, he was so earnest—I loved his emotional openness. One day Tony said, "I think that I would like to be a psychologist, but I could never be as calm as you. My friends like to come to me and tell me about their problems, but I can't control myself. I have to tell people how I feel." Smiling warmly I said, "You have a big heart and a great capacity for empathy. I think that you would make a good psychologist."

A few months before he consulted me, Tony's beloved aunt had died. Aunt Tina had lived with his family since Tony was two years old. He was twenty-six now. He had spent a lot of time caring for her in recent years as she slowly started to fade. Because of her weakened condition, he had not taken any vacation time in over a year. He wanted to spend as much time as possible helping to take care of her. However, he also wanted to visit some boyhood friends who now lived in Detroit. He shared his dilemma with his mother. She reassured him that the doctor had said that his aunt was stable and would probably live at least six more months. His mother gave him permission to go. On the fifth day of his trip Tony called home. His mother answered the phone and told him his aunt had taken a sudden downturn and was spiraling quickly toward death. Tony started driving toward home immediately. Aunt Tina died while he was on the road. He felt tremendously guilty that he wasn't there for her at the end of her life and that he didn't get to say good-bye and thank her for all she had done for him.

Since he and Aunt Tina had such a powerful, loving connection, I suggested to Tony that he could have a heart-to-heart conversation with her asking for forgiveness. Tony responded, "I know she forgives me. As we are talking I am realizing that what really needs to happen is that I need to forgive myself. How do I do that?" Frequently in our talks, Tony would say fervently about some friend or family member, "I love him to death," revealing the depth of his capacity to love. Yet, he tended to be hard on himself and struggled mightily with the notions of loving himself and accepting his human limitations. I told Tony, "You are a powerful lover. I have no doubt that you love deeply and that the people in your life know that and feel your heart energy. Imagine if that loving energy went outward from your heart and made a 180 degree turn and came back toward you." I extended my right hand out from my heart, and then turned it slowly toward myself. "Imagine that your heart holds for you the same loving and compassionate energy that it holds for others." I asked Tony to imagine holding his own heart toward himself as I described that loving energy returning to him and filling him with forgiveness. Tony started to cry. We used the gesture of Tony holding his heart and turning its loving focus toward himself for several sessions. In between he worked with the prayer *Help me to forgive myself.* As a result of that work not only did he know that his Aunt Tina forgave him, but he also was able to forgive himself.

Most of my sessions with Tony were focused on his dependence on marijuana—he usually wore a Grateful Dead t-shirt to our meetings— and his inability to fall in love or let women love him. On some level he felt that he didn't deserve to have a good life. The reason for this became clear one night when Tony walked in and began our conversation by saying solemnly that his buddies had died on this date seven years earlier. I felt so grateful at that moment that the patient scheduled after him had cancelled just an hour before. Tony would be my last patient that evening—we could take as much time as he needed.

To commemorate their death, Tony usually would go to the cemetery and spend the night hanging out with his dead friends. He would be going there after our session. I asked him to tell me some of the details of the accident. "We always hung out together and got high. But that night, some voice inside me said to stay home. I would usually have been the driver, but Sean was at the wheel instead. He always drove fast. He lost control of the car only a few blocks from his home." Two other friends died instantly, but Sean lived for a little while. His sister and mother told Tony that when the emergency medical team pulled him out of the wreck, Sean's final words were, "I really fucked up this time." Tony started to cry.

As I listened to Tony's story, I thought about other times I had helped patients with issues related to loved ones who had died. Years ago I had accompanied a teenage patient and his mother to a group session with a well-respected medium. They were hoping to make contact with the boy's dead father. While that did not happen, I witnessed the medium make connections with the deceased loved ones of a number of people in the room. Again and again, the message that the medium reported was about forgiveness—people "on the other side" need to feel forgiven by those still living, and the living need to ask forgiveness from the ones who have passed on. I have read this same thing in a number of books and have heard similar accounts from a couple of friends who have attended these sessions with similarly well-respected mediums.

I decided to share this story with Tony that night. "Perhaps when you go to the cemetery tonight you can have a conversation with your friends, especially Sean." Tony began to cry harder. I explained that this kind of conversation, between one heart and another, doesn't need to make rational sense. "What would I talk about?" Tony asked. "Well," I replied, "It seems to me there are two parts. From what you've told me, Sean would probably want to ask your forgiveness for fucking up and causing so much pain for you and so many other people." Tony replied, "That sounds right, except I don't blame him. I love him so much, I'm not angry at him."

I reiterated for Tony what the medium had said. "Sean needs to hear from you that you forgive him. He felt responsible for fucking up." The second part I told Tony, was about what he needed to say to Sean. "That's easy," Tony said, "I need to tell Sean I am sorry I wasn't in the car with him that night." Tony looked momentarily confused. "But, I'm also glad that I listened to that inner voice and didn't go. How do I reconcile that?"

I reassured Tony that it is completely normal to have two opposite feelings coexisting inside of him. "Maybe what you need to say to Sean is, *Please forgive me for not riding with you that night and being with you. Please forgive me for being glad that I'm still alive. Is it OK with you that I'm still alive?*" Tony said, "It would be OK with him." I replied, "Yeah, but maybe you need to ask him." Tony nodded as we both just sat quietly crying. After a time, Tony said, "I have a lot to talk about with him tonight." I nodded, "Why don't we stop and you go have your talk." We hugged and he left.

Tony's story illustrates additional ways in which I use imagery and an expansion of the idea of "prayer." Particularly with people who are easily compassionate and forgiving of others and hard on themselves, I find it helpful to have them imagine their own heart outside of themselves. I suggest that this "big heart," so capable of accepting the limitations of others, has enough love and compassion to penetrate the layers of their feeling unworthy of forgiveness. I have them imagine rays of forgiving energy radiating from their big heart and penetrating deeply into their small, physical heart. Doing this imagery during sessions and encouraging patients to use it between sessions increases their openness and receptivity to forgiving themselves.

For patients like Tony, who have some unfinished forgiveness work with someone who has died, I have found it to be quite helpful to share the anecdotes of well-respected mediums about the issue of forgiveness for those "on the other side." Most people, I find, are very open to the idea of communicating heart-to-heart or soul-to-soul. By simply expanding on the prayer, *Please forgive me*, I will have my patient imagine a fuller conversation with the deceased person, a part of which eventually includes asking for forgiveness. It is important in doing this work to allow the sense of being forgiven by the other to emerge in its own time.

THERAPIST, HEAL THYSELF

We often need to forgive ourselves because we have failed to live up to our own self-expectations: we are unable to be the mother or father we would like to be, we stumbled again in dealing with an old habit or addiction, we did not stick to a diet or to a more disciplined exercise regimen, we again failed to be the kind of loving partner we want to be, or we screwed up in our work.

As psychotherapists, we, too, need to forgive ourselves for mistakes we have made. Most of the therapists I know—including myself—carry unrealistically high expectations of themselves. When we do or say something that is not helpful or causes pain for a patient, a particular kind of self-denigration or self-attack often occurs: *How could I have said or done that? I don't know anything. I am a fraud. Maybe I shouldn't be a therapist.* At different times in my thirty-five year journey as a psychotherapist, I have experienced some variation of these doubts and self-accusations. These moments have taught me the importance of us as therapists being able to forgive ourselves and developing a more compassionate and gentle attitude for the inevitable mistakes that we make. The more we are able to forgive ourselves for our own human limitations, the more we will be able to be a compassionate guide for our patients in their struggles with their own unrealistic expectations.

Obviously, the issue of self-criticalness is complex, has many sources and does not apply only to psychotherapists. As therapists each of us needs to explore honestly and deeply the roots of our own personal expectations and the reason for particular errors. Sometimes we experience simply a temporary human state such as tiredness, irritability or preoccupation with some personal life issue that interferes with our ability to be present. Sometimes a personality characteristic of a patient triggers something in our history. Recently, I was reminded that I struggle with patients who need to be right. Clearly that resonates with my father's pattern of always needing to be right. It was his way or not at all. During my meditation recently, I started laughing at myself, recognizing that I too need to be right, far more often than I am consciously aware. And, of course, I said long ago that I would never be like my father! My laughter at myself is reflective of a well-developed inner voice of self-forgiveness that says—*Even with all your years of experience you are still vulnerable to these transference issues. Be gentle with yourself, laugh at yourself, forgive yourself for being human.*

One of the dangers of being an elder therapist is hubris! Sometimes I think that I *know* what a patient needs and fall into the role of expert. This was revealed to me again on my weekly walk in the woods. At the beginning of my walk, I take a few moments to focus my intention on connecting with other creatures, to the Creator and to my Higher Self. Although I usually start out with a destination in mind, I try to remain open to what beckons me. On this early winter day, I found myself drifting toward a cascade of flowing water. I stopped alongside this small waterfall and closed my eyes. Unexpectedly, I started to speak aloud and found myself asking a patient to forgive me for not being helpful. "Forgive me for not really listening. My ego got in the way of helping you." Two months before, a patient had stopped treatment after six sessions. On reflection, I realized that my own self-image as an expert had interfered with a basic treatment adage: to take the patient where he or she is, and not presume that I know best what to do.

I had been beating myself up for weeks about this failure. As I stood by the cascade, I began to imagine the water flowing over me. There was snow on the ground and some of the cascade was frozen. Otherwise I would have taken off my shoes and put my feet into the water. I stood for quite a while listening and imagining myself under the falling water being cleansed. I imagined my Higher Self forgiving me, saying: *You are only human. Even though you have many years of experience you still make mistakes. You did not help him, but you did not harm him. Forgive yourself. You did not live up to your own expectations. Even the most experienced therapists make mistakes.*

It felt to me that my Higher Self had guided me to this cascading water. As I stood there, I recalled that many years earlier, during my very dark period, I had used images of brooks, cascades and the ocean and imagined letting the water run over me. Now as then, my Higher Self was guiding me to create an inner ritual to help me forgive myself.

Immersion in water or the pouring of water over a person is an ancient and ubiquitous ritual of forgiveness. For example, it is at the core of the Christian ritual of baptism, when the soul is cleansed of its sins so that it can be born anew. The psychological equivalent is to forgive ourselves for past errors or woundings so that we can be reborn into a fuller, more compassionate and loving self. Frequently water images emerge spontaneously for patients and sometimes I will suggest them as a way of evoking that collective memory. At the end of an intensive men's retreat several years ago, I had the men pair up and ritually wash the feet of the other as he meditated on something he needed forgiveness for. My experience at the waterfall reminds me of the importance of creating meaningful rituals of forgiveness. Sometimes, as in the men's retreat, we can use a form of ritual that we know from our own or some other spiritual tradition. At other times, if we remain open and receptive, our Higher Self will create a forgiveness ritual for us.

UNCONSCIOUS GUILT

As I am thinking about how to conclude this chapter on self-forgiveness, my mind returns to the time of dark depression and despair in my own life. Jeanne and some of my psychologist friends recommended that I see a therapist. Did I listen? Of course not. I was suicidal (which I did not disclose to Jeanne or my friends) and yet I was not seeking help. After several months, I finally sought out my old analyst. He helped me see that at some level of consciousness, I felt unworthy or undeserving of having a good life and that the degree of guilt I was experiencing was disproportionate to what had happened. He suggested that there was probably something more, something unconscious that was making my guilt so big. Gradually, he helped me to understand the unconscious part of my guilt. Remember, I was a person who didn't cause pain for other people, especially the ones I love most. Yet I had disconnected from the parts of me that had been wounded again and again by my wife's frequent criticalness. I was out of touch with my anger and the extent to which her criticism had eroded my feelings of self-worth. By causing her such great pain through my leaving without warning, I had exacted my revenge. Of course, I wasn't aware of this at the time, only understanding it as I examined the depths of my guilt layer by layer.

This experience taught me a lot about the power and insidious nature of unconscious guilt. My guilt got me to make financial concessions in our divorce agreement that caused raised eyebrows among my closest friends. Unconscious guilt made me feel undeserving of a good life and, at times, suicidal. While my analyst was helpful in bringing me to the insight about my unconscious guilt, he was clueless about the territory of self-forgiveness. As the director of a psychoanalytic institute and the author of several books, he was a national figure in the field. Yet he had reached the limits of his knowledge and experience. As a traditional Freudian analyst, he did not believe in introducing spirituality into the psychotherapy process because of his concern about contaminating the therapy with his own religious values. Nor did he have any knowledge about how to actively engage the heart realms through the use of images of compassion. This left me on my own. Yet this time, I knew what to do. I returned to the woods and sat down again under the giant old pines that I had named "momma" and "poppa." I used my images of Jesus and Buddha, and said my prayers, *Forgive me, help me to forgive myself.* I asked my dead parents for help, *Please help your son.* During this time I also went back to my image of the cascade and imagined the water flowing over me, washing away my guilt, recreating my own self-forgiveness ritual. Sometimes I felt a comforting presence. Gradually my heart became lighter, my spirit freer—I felt forgiven once again.

SELF-FORGIVENESS IN EVERYDAY LIFE

My own experience with forgiving myself was a powerful teacher. It showed me that the work of self-forgiveness is mysterious, non-rational, non-linear and unpredictable. Our task is to engage ourselves consciously in the process, to be open to its unfolding and trust that something outside our ordinary selves is helping and guiding us. It also taught me the ongoing nature of self-forgiveness. The stories in this chapter have been about major life events for which Ralph, Michelle, Tony and I needed forgiveness. What about the lesser moments of everyday life when the critical and judgmental parts of our personality cause periods of self-anger, disappointment, loathing, depression and self-recrimination? These parts of ourselves can create havoc in our inner landscape, contaminate our day and intrude into our relationships.

Once my patients have experienced the process of forgiving themselves for some major issue, it becomes easier for them to access that process with smaller issues. When something is raised during a session, I'll suggest to my patients that they use the forgiveness prayer cards during the period before our next session. Often they share with me that they keep the cards in some private place. Others say that they don't need the cards because they readily remember the words. For some patients, I rewrite the forgiveness prayers that connected for them in the past. At the next session my patients usually report that working with the prayers between meetings has already begun to diminish their guilt. I encourage them to continue. When needed, we will do some additional forgiveness imagery for a few sessions. With each experience, the forgiving part of the Self becomes a stronger and more accessible voice in our inner landscape. After a while it just shows up unbidden, and either quiets down or counteracts the critical, guilt-inducing parts of our personality.

Healthy guilt that comes from a fully formed conscience is an essential part of our human experience. It helps us to know when we have caused harm or wronged another person. We will invariably cause pain to others. We always need to forgive ourselves no matter what we have done. Unhealthy guilt, on the other hand, is always out of proportion to the offense, usually weighs us down for long periods of time without any feeling of resolution, is not relieved through cognitive insights or making amends and is more connected to our core feelings about ourselves than to what we have actually done. Forgiveness in these situations seems impossible. Even more insidious is when we are not even conscious that we are feeling guilty. Instead we act in ways that are clearly self-sabotaging or self-destructive and reveal some deep, underlying feelings of personal unworthiness. This kind of guilt, especially, needs the softness of our emotional hearts and the compassion of self-forgiveness.

My own personal experiences and years of working with patients on these issues offer a beacon of hope. These experiences have shown me that everyone and everything is forgiveable. It is essential for us, as therapists, to encourage our patients to actively engage in the process of forgiving themselves and then help them to persist, trusting that the process of forgiving themselves will unfold in its own timetable, in ways that are unique for each person.

③

UPROOTING THE IMPLANTS

Many of us carry within us feeling states that do not belong to us. Yet we think they do. Sometimes it is a deep sadness, or a general fearfulness about life, or easily triggered anger or an anxiety about money or a pessimistic worldview. Yet when I explore with patients their current life or personal history, the depth of this feeling state and its intransigence does not fit. It is as if something has been implanted in his or her psyche that does not belong there. Nonetheless, it feels to the patient as if this is "who I am" and she will say with certainty, "I am a fearful (depressed, pessimistic, etc.) person, and I can't change that." What is remarkable about these states is their stubbornness. Despite the fact that, rationally, they do not make sense in the context of the patient's personhood or life experience, the feeling state holds on, refusing to leave. It is deeply rooted.

Although what I am describing is related to concepts like "introject" and "internalization," patients experience these states as less defined than an internalized "voice" or parental "image." It is as if the emotional atmosphere in the family creates a particular landscape in the home. Then, over time, seeds from the family landscape are carried in the atmosphere of the home and make their way into the internal landscape of the child. The metaphor that came to me early in my practice is something I remember from high school biology. The membrane of our cells is permeable and therefore something from the outside can easily flow through the membrane into the cell. Comparably, for infants and young children the membrane of the self is vulnerable, and not well formed; it too is permeable. Young children have trouble differentiating what is *me* and what is *not me*. If a parent or some other significant person in the child's family is often depressed, fearful, angry or highly anxious, the energetic vibration of that frequent feeling state can enter into the child and become *implanted* inside the self-in-formation. The more sensitive the child, the more likely the state will be internalized. The more exposure the child has to that person, the more that feeling state can become entrenched. The earlier in childhood that these experiences occur, the more it will feel like *this is who I am*. The more the child is deeply emotionally attached to the original carrier of this feeling state, the more deeply rooted it will become. For some patients this feeling state is always present; it is their "normal." For many others it is dormant and lurking underground until some life event awakens it and the state becomes activated.

Increasingly I utilize metaphors from nature to explain psychological processes to patients. When I talk about this particular process, I tell them how these feeling states are "implanted" inside us and how deeply rooted they become. Like invasive weeds in a garden, they crowd the good seeds and hinder our growth. I explain that these implants need to be uprooted, pulled out. Because they are so deeply rooted, they do not come out easily or quickly. I encourage patients to visualize an inner garden, imagining these implants as the weeds. I have them imagine yanking them out while also taking some deep breaths. Whenever they notice this unwanted feeling state showing up, I encourage them to practice this visualization and breathing for five or ten minutes or until they begin to notice that the feeling state diminishes for the time being.

WAYNE

Wayne is a psychotherapist who has been a patient of mine for several years. Recently, he was talking about his high anxiety because he had a number of openings in his schedule and many patients had cancelled sessions in the previous month. Wayne talked about not having enough money to pay his bills; how his income was lower than in previous years and how difficult things were financially, especially since his wife was not working. She was at home caring for their infant son. That morning, when she mentioned that they needed a new dishwasher, he had said to her angrily, "Don't you realize that we're broke?" Since I know very well the recurrent anxieties that come with the territory of being a self-employed therapist, it was easy for me to be compassionate about his emotional state. I also knew for a fact that Wayne and his wife were far from broke. After a moment, I said teasingly, "Of course, you do own two homes (he rents out a place for extra income) and just got back from a vacation in Las Vegas." Wayne burst into laughter. He realized that he was overreacting, that the phrase, "we're broke" did not fit their current life situation. He was then open to exploring the historical roots of his feeling state.

Wayne was the last of ten children in a working class family. In school he felt that he was the poorest kid in his class and lived in dread of other kids discovering this. He recalled his humiliation when other kids made fun of his unmatched socks or frequent peanut butter sandwiches for lunch. To Wayne, these were markers that his family was poor. His parents did not view themselves as working class, but rather as poor, and they were ashamed of their financial status. Whenever he or his siblings would ask for school supplies or some toy they saw other kids playing with, his father would become enraged, shouting, "We're broke!" "Broke" was the code word for poor.

As we explored further, Wayne recalled that his grandparents were Polish peasants who came to America to escape real poverty. They started small businesses that eventually collapsed during the Great Depression. The family really struggled to put food on the table. Recalling this helped Wayne to understand the bigness of his emotional reaction to these intermittent thoughts that his practice would fail and he wouldn't be able to support his family—even though he had maintained a successful practice for over ten years. It helped him to understand why none of his siblings had ever tried to have their own business despite the fact that a number of them were excellent carpenters and electricians. The roots of this implant of financial anxiety and the fear of poverty went back several generations in Wayne's family. It was a feeling state that, even when it wasn't talked about, was in the atmosphere of his childhood home. He had carried this feeling for most of his fifty-four years. When I described to him the metaphor of uprooting this implant, Wayne immediately thought of his wife's garden. He thought about how often she would be outside weeding and how tenacious some of the weeds could be. He liked the metaphor and was eager to begin using it as a tool.

After awakening from a dream the night before a session with Wayne, I was reminded of my own implanted fears about poverty. I dreamed that a rat had gotten into my office. I hissed at it like a cat and growled at it like a dog, but I couldn't drive it away. In fact, it got bigger and then hid somewhere in my office. Talking over coffee the next morning with my wife, Jeanne, it became clear to me that the rat symbolized poverty. Working with Wayne on his fears of being broke had restimulated my own fears. Even though years of therapy and spiritual practice had greatly diminished my anxiety about money, the "rat" still lived in the shadow of my unconscious. Like Wayne, there was nothing in my current life situation to justify the fear. I had come to understand its rootedness in generations of struggling Irish farmers, poor immigrant grandparents and my own parents downward mobility in their working class world. This powerful psychic energy, implanted early on, could still reemerge in my dreams. I doubt it will ever completely go away.

Some of these implants are more deeply rooted and more complex than they initially appear. Wayne understood this viscerally as he recalled an experience of he and his wife digging out an old rhododendron in her garden. The job was much more difficult than they had anticipated. As he dug down, he could see multiple, interwoven root systems: small roots just under the surface intertwined with thicker roots more deeply buried. Some seemed to wrap around the roots of other plants. The main root was quite deep. The smaller roots Wayne and his wife could simply pull out. Then they needed clippers. For some thicker roots he used a large pruning tool. To remove the deep root he tied a rope to the rear bumper of his SUV and yanked it out. It didn't come out easily. He felt this was an apt metaphor for the continuing work of ridding himself of the "poverty implant."

As was true in my own family and was also true for Wayne, oftentimes these implanted emotional states have intergenerational roots. This became clearer to Wayne as he recalled how his mother would hide bills from his father. At the same time, she was afraid they wouldn't be able to pay them. He remembered her often saying, "We're going to lose our home."

Wayne's mother had grown up in the midst of the Depression. She carried her family's personal history of a cataclysmic collective event that is at the root of so many people's implanted anxiety about money and poverty. In her case, her father had been a successful businessman until the Depression, when he went bankrupt and soon lost the family home. He never fully recovered from these devastating events. With more business failures later on, the family moved repeatedly from one apartment to another. As Wayne recalled, his mother told him "millions of stories about the Depression," including the story of how she was sent to the railroad yard to collect stray pieces of coal that had fallen from the coal cars. She would bring them home for the family to use as fuel. The memories of those times must have left a powerful imprint on Wayne's mother. She was probably frightened of ever returning to those times.

Wayne, a sensitive child who was quite close to his mother, was vulnerable to this repetitive message of impending financial doom. The highly anxious energy of his mother easily overwhelmed the porous membrane of his developing self. His frequent exposure to his mother's fearfulness about money thickened and deepened the roots of this implant.

Wayne's father also passed on his intergenerational implant about poverty. As I mentioned, Wayne's grandparents on his father's side were Polish immigrants who left Poland to escape poverty. Whenever he heard them speak about life in Poland, the strongest feeling that came across was a sense of shame and humiliation about being poor. Although his father rarely revealed his feelings, Wayne could sense that he carried this same shame about his own family's financial situation. Yet it was not accurate; they were not poor, they were working class. Wayne's father was a semi-skilled man who worked steadily for the same construction company for thirty years. He managed to provide adequately for his wife and ten children. The emotional implant of the shame of his parents' life in Poland did not fit in the United States. This too was passed on to his sensitive son. Wayne is a carrier of the family shame, still afraid he cannot provide for his own family, even though he has a thriving practice and owns a home and a rental property.

Wayne defines himself as a "worrier." As we continued our work of up-rooting this emotional implant, I was able to help Wayne redefine himself as a *warrior*. "Think of the *warrior*," I suggested, "as the one who is up-rooting the *worrier*." He enjoyed the playfulness of that use of language. As a psychotherapist, Wayne was also familiar with the Jungian notions of archetype and collective unconscious. So the way we conceptualized it was that he was drawing upon the collective unconscious to awaken the ancient archetype of the *warrior* to assist him with this tenacious implant. He developed a visual image of a Native American warrior who used his considerable strength to pull out the roots of his implants.

JACK AND KATIE

In the aftermath of Hurricane Katrina, several people from New Orleans moved into our area. Looking for a way to help, I offered my services as a psychotherapist without charge to anyone in need. Shortly thereafter, a very interesting couple in their mid-thirties called me and we met seven or eight times. One day Jack and Katie announced that they had decided to return to New Orleans. Jack, however, was sure that everything would go wrong and prevent them from leaving.

Because they had been through an extreme trauma, I first explored Jack's reaction in relationship to their experience in Katrina. But quickly, Kate made it clear that this was nothing new for Jack; he always reacted to things in this way. "I'm a pessimist," Jack said, "that's just who I am." I replied, "Perhaps you have a part of you that is pessimistic, Jack. These parts are never the totality of who we are. In fact, in my experience, this kind of pervasive worldview is often something that really doesn't be-long to us at all, but is passed on to us from one of our parents." I talked with Jack and Katie about the idea of implanted emotional states. "Do you think this might be true for you Jack?" I asked.

Kate could barely contain herself. "Oh boy, if you ever met his mother!" Jack then described his mother as "pessimistic and paranoid." This perva-sive and omnipresent feeling state emanated from his mother throughout his childhood. People, she insisted, could not be trusted, and because of that, bad things were going to happen to you. She lived in a malevolent universe and she transmitted that to her children. Although the catastrophe of Katrina might reinforce this worldview, Jack's overall life experience did not bear this out. The idea that this pessimism was implanted from his mother made sense to Jack. Kate, who had many years of frustration trying to constructively counter Jack's perspective, compared it to a virus that needed an antibiotic. Jack, a poet and writer, liked the notion of uprooting the implant, immediately conjuring an image of the trees around his New Orleans home: though you could see some of the roots above the ground, mostly they went deeply below the surface. He could see himself already pulling and tugging at the roots of his pessimism.

In Jack's case, because this pessimistic part of him was so pervasive and I wanted him to begin to experience it as a *part* of himself rather than the totality, I suggested that he come up with a name that would personify his pessimism.

"Frenchy," Jack said almost immediately. "My mother is French, this comes from her, so . . ."

I suggested that he and Kate use "Frenchy" in a playful way—not judgmentally—to remind Jack when he was identified with that implanted emotional state. I reminded them both that we work at uprooting these implants over a lifetime. As the roots became less embedded "Frenchy's" appearances would be less frequent.

As we were finishing our brief work together, Jack was fantasizing about going home to New Orleans and having a po' boy at their favorite restaurant. "But it probably won't even be there anymore. Or the po' boys won't be good."

"Frenchy," Kate said, smiling and rolling her eyes, "have you forgotten that we went online and found out that the place is still there and open for business?" And I said teasingly, "Yeah, but the meat will probably be poisoned!" We laughed heartily, acknowledging playfully that mom's "paranoid and pessimistic" outlook had shown up again. With greater insight and some new psychological tools, Jack and Kate returned home to New Orleans.

CARL

Sometimes an implant is subtle in its influence and it takes a while in the therapy before it reveals itself. Early in our process, I had taught

Carl the relaxation technique that I refer to throughout this book to help with his anxiety. Often during sessions he would take a few moments to focus on his breathing. When this occurred Carl would mention how his neck and shoulders would feel more relaxed and his chest felt more expansive. During one session he started to cry, saying, "I feel that a tightness around my heart is loosening up." This led to a discussion of how he did not feel open to emotional closeness with his wife. If she sat next to him, Carl could feel his body constricting—sometimes he would move over. He realized that his heart was not open to freely receiving and giving love. As he talked, I suggested that he continue to focus on his breathing and notice whatever memories came up that would help us to understand why.

Carl began to talk about the atmosphere in his childhood home. His mother and grandmother, who lived in an upstairs apartment, were very judgmental. And fearful. He also described an inner city, all boys' Catholic high school where he felt like an outsider. Carl felt intimidated by the athletic and intellectual competitiveness that was in the air. Both at home and in school, he shut down. He mentioned that his grandmother was an immigrant who had escaped from the oppression of a communist regime in Czechoslovakia. She also felt persecuted when she first entered the United States. She passed on to Carl's mother her sense that the world is a scary, malevolent place where people want to harm you. The sense of profound fearfulness that they carried in their consciousness permeated the atmosphere of Carl's childhood home. Because he was a sensitive boy, this fearful energy easily penetrated the permeable membranes of Carl's developing sense of self. The competitive atmosphere of high school only reinforced the family perspective of the world as a threatening, unsafe place.

Carl is aware that he has some psychic abilities. As an acupuncturist, he periodically has intuitions about his clients that are almost always accurate. This ability both intrigues and frightens him. When he revealed some of this ability as a boy, his mother and grandmother would sternly say, "Stop that, it's evil!" From his grandmother's Eastern European peasant background, any psychic abilities were interpreted as evidence of the presence of evil spirits aligned with the devil. With that kind of admonition, Carl quickly learned to shut down that part of himself.

I interpreted to Carl that in his current life, whenever he started to open his heart or tried to be receptive to his psychic gifts, there was something inside that made him feel his openness was unsafe, that malevolent people or forces would harm him. I also told him that this inner sense was implanted by both his mother and grandmother and that it did not fit the world in which he was living. It was generational and probably preceded his grandmother. For Carl to evolve as an acupuncturist and healer, it was necessary for him to diminish the power of these implants. For him to be more open-hearted so that he could more freely receive and give love, it was essential to loosen the grip of his fear and self-judgment. My description of how the process of implanting works made a lot of sense to him.

In the next session, Carl reported that he had been using the breathing technique as a way of releasing the physiological constriction that he felt in his body and letting go of the psychological state of fearfulness. He also asked if there were something more he could do to free himself of this implant. I remembered that in addition to doing traditional acupuncture, he was also developing his skills in other methods of energy healing. I suggested to Carl that he think of the judgmentalness and fearfulness as unwanted energetic entities that he is releasing because they don't belong to him. "Sometimes you might even address them," I said, "You might say, '*Go away. You do not belong inside of me. You belong to someone else.*'" Carl liked this notion; it fit his psychic experience of sensing energetic "presences" in his work with his own clients. Because Carl did not yet feel powerful enough to combat them alone, I told him to think of me standing alongside him as he worked with these energy states. The image of my supportive presence helped ward off the fearfulness.

I offered myself to Carl as an ally in his inner world. Within his family constellation there was no strong presence to counteract the prevailing atmospheric energy of fear. So there was no model of how to maintain a sense of self that could ward off the fear. For a while he borrowed my strength. Within the office he would witness how I responded to the fearful energy that he carried in his consciousness and gradually began to internalize that kind of peaceful, loving and compassionate presence. In between our sessions he would visualize me standing alongside him whenever the powerful fearfulness would flow through him, remembering how I was in our face-to-face encounters, and he would breathe out the negative energy. Carl described the physiological changes that he was experiencing as his breathing became less constricted and his heart rate slowed down, and how he felt freer psychologically. After a few months he stopped using my image because he no longer needed to draw strength from me.

Since his mid-twenties Carl intermittently had read about consciousness and how it was possible to transcend ordinary states of consciousness. Although he had explored this territory intellectually he had never seriously investigated any practices that would help him to engage those realms within himself. When I queried him about the reasons for this, it became clear that his grandmother's labeling of those energetic states as evil and evidence of the devil's influence made Carl quite afraid of further exploration. After we worked through that concern, I discussed with him the notion of the Higher Self. He was intrigued and receptive to developing some connection to that part of himself. Initially, we explored this in the safety of the office. With his eyes closed, after several minutes of focused breathing, I suggested to Carl that he simply be open and receptive to whatever image came into his consciousness. No particular form showed up. What he experienced instead was a benevolent, loving, energetic presence. This was in sharp contrast to the malevolent image of dark, frightening forces that were described by his mother and grandmother. This was the kind of presence that he had needed all his life. As Carl increasingly connected with this aspect of his own consciousness, he was able to release more and more of the fear-filled implant.

MAUREEN

Some of my patients live with the constant anticipation that something bad is going to happen. For a few, the sense is omnipresent; for most it is an undercurrent that gushes easily to the surface. Usually some life event—a medical test, a financial setback, some uncertainty in a job or relationship—taps into this subconscious feeling state and then dread or panic overflows into consciousness. Patients experience this anticipatory dread viscerally as the vibration of anxious energy takes over their bodies. These patients have had bad things happen in their lives, sometimes a lot of bad things. Yet there is generally something else, something more foundational that underlies these negative life experiences. With other experiences added on top, the feeling state becomes more entrenched, more rooted.

One of Maureen's most endearing qualities was the earnestness with which she approached her therapy and recovery. A recovering alcoholic in her mid-fifties, she went to meetings at least twice a week, checked in with her sponsor every day, kept a daily journal that included writing down her dreams, had a stack of recovery literature on her bedside table and thought a lot about what we had discussed in the previous week's therapy. Her psychological healing was the most important thing in her life and she pursued it diligently. In the second year of our work, Maureen became increasingly aware that she was always "waiting for the other shoe to drop." That was her normal state. Even when things were going well, she was unable to relax and enjoy the moment. Whenever life presented her with a setback or even the possibility of something negative, she went into a survival mode of preparedness, anticipating the worst. Instead of becoming paralyzed by the anxiety, however, as some others might react, Maureen became mobilized. Her mind would be filled with possible solutions to the problem and she would take any action to control the situation. At work this made her a valued executive. At home, however, her need for control would make her easily angered and she was often oppressive with her husband and two teenage daughters. Since her teens she had used alcohol as a way of controlling her anxiety and warding off panic. Now that she had stopped drinking she was feeling the anxiety more and in some ways her home life had worsened. This made her exceptionally motivated to change.

There were two primary historical sources of Maureen's anticipatory anxiety. One was that Maureen's mother was also an alcoholic. When she wasn't drinking she was affectionate and fun to be around. When she was drinking, she would either become withdrawn or attack Maureen's appearance and intelligence mercilessly. As her mother's drinking progressed, these daily fluctuations in mood became more extreme. As a result, Maureen could never relax at home. Even when her mother was in a pleasant mood, she was always "waiting for the other shoe to drop."

After work, Maureen's father would wait anxiously, wondering if his wife had stopped for drinks on her way home. He would forewarn

Maureen not to do anything that would irritate her mother. This sense of anxious dread was always in the atmosphere. Now, as Maureen thought about it, her father's sense of foreboding seemed exaggerated. Her mother's moods weren't that bad, she wasn't explosive or physically abusive. She didn't create a lot of big fights. Maureen began to wonder if there was some other reason that her father always seemed to be expecting the worst.

As often happens with these implants, Maureen's father's catastrophic thinking had its own historical roots. She remembered him talking fondly of his parents and how they described the beauty of the Irish countryside with its green pastures and stone walls. These stories were always tainted, however, by memories of the extreme poverty and political persecution experienced by his parents and grandparents. Maureen recalled listening to these stories and the sense of sadness and suffering that loomed around her father. He was a gifted storyteller and Maureen had absorbed his sense of dread that the worst was about to happen.

Maureen appreciated my explanation of how these implants develop, but my metaphor of *uprooting* did not connect for her. As a person who loved to walk along the seashore and woodland streams, she preferred to use the image of moving water to help rid herself of these unwanted feeling states. At some sessions she would imagine sitting by the ocean, allowing the incoming waves to enter her consciousness, take up the anxious anticipation of bad things happening and carry it away with the ebbing waves. At other times she would imagine a brook flowing inside of her, cleansing the dread and carrying it downstream. When she added some breath work to her imagery, she could feel a physiological release of the anxious energy. Her breathing and heart rate slowed. She felt more at peace.

Of course through her recovery work in AA, Maureen was very familiar with the concept of Higher Power. However, she never felt a sense of connectedness to her own personal Higher Power. Through our work, she imagined that part of herself as Rebecca, a loving, strong, although not loud, voice from within that periodically showed up to offer wise counsel. Usually when the implant of impending doom and gloom was dominating Maureen's inner world, Rebecca would show up and say, "That was then and this is now. When you were a girl, bad things were happening frequently. You could never allow yourself to relax. Now you can, that time is over. Just breathe and let go of the feeling of dread."

During my years of experience there have been several patients who didn't connect to the language of uprooting the implants. They thought that my description of the process of implanting was useful, but the notion of uprooting was dissonant for them. So, we found alternative pathways of accomplishing the same therapeutic goal. One patient, who had a scientific background, preferred to imagine that when he took his morning aspirin for his heart condition, the pill was dissolving into his blood stream, clearing out the familial shame that contaminated his inner landscape. It was helpful. In one session he talked about the research that demonstrated the efficacy of the placebo effect. "If I believe it is beneficial medicine for getting rid of that shame," he said, "then it will work."

Another patient, whose work involved developing computer programs, also found the language of uprooting too alien to his world. So he used the conceptual framework that I had presented and adapted a method that fit for him. He described it this way: "I love the *delete* key on my computer. I get so many e-mails that I don't want to read. There is such a feeling of power in being able to push *delete* and this unwanted stuff is just wiped out." Whenever his familial implant of judgmentalness showed up, he imagined pushing the *delete* key and did the releasing breathing. That worked for him.

(4)

THE COUNCIL

Inevitably at some point in the process of their psychotherapy each patient presents some complex life dilemma, the resolution of which will result in a significant life change. During this time the person experiences a lot of inner tension and confusion because several parts of the personality have very different, often opposing, feelings and thoughts about what to do. Here are a few examples: the woman who has decided to end her marriage and learns her husband has cancer; the divorced coach who has been offered his "dream job" in another part of the country away from his children; the single career woman who has inherited a lot of money and wonders about adopting a child; the priest who has been offered a highly prestigious position in the church yet is awakened in the middle of the night by dreams of being a father.

I tell patients that these big dilemmas cannot be resolved at the level of consciousness at which they currently exist. A good resolution that answers the essential question *What is in my best interest in this situation?* cannot come from a rational approach. Making lists of the pros and cons does not work. Trying to respond to the conflict simply from a pragmatic or moral perspective only increases the confusion and inner tension. From my thirty-five years of experience in sitting with patients struggling with these dilemmas, I think that they are best resolved from the realm of the heart and by engaging the Higher Self as a source of inner wisdom.

Initially patients are both confused and intrigued when I explain my thinking about this process. I tell them that what they experience as *conflict* are the thoughts and feelings that are emanating from several distinct parts of their personality. These different parts, some conscious and others unconscious, are in a state of *dynamic tension*. I explain that most people, because they cannot tolerate the level of ongoing anxiety and uncertainty, usually make a hasty decision by favoring one part of the personality over the others. These premature decisions are often a mistake. Either the other parts of the personality continue to create tension and undermine the decision or the issue becomes submerged only to resurface a few months or a few years later.

I offer my patients the metaphor of "the Council" as an alternative pathway toward a resolution of these big issues. From the perspective of a higher level of consciousness, it provides a way to value, with compassion and nonjudgment, the thoughts and feelings of each part of the personality so that each can contribute toward a resolution that is in the best interest of the whole person. This usually results in some answer that no one part could have come to on its own. The Council also provides a container for all the conflicting feelings so that the dynamic tension of the dilemma can be tolerated for an extended period of time.

When I first started to utilize the Council, I found it helpful to think of myself as a group therapist or facilitator, with different parts of the same person, rather than a number of different people as the group members. In this way I was utilizing a skill that I already had and transferring it to this model. This reduced my uncertainty about being on unfamiliar ground and gave me an opportunity to experiment with this process with a greater sense of ease.

INITIATING A COUNCIL

When I do this work first I ask my patient to imagine that all the different parts of their personality have decided to have a meeting to explore their particular issue. I ask the person to imagine the kind of physical setting in which this gathering would occur and I give them some examples of settings other people have used.

Sometimes people select a favorite nature setting and imagine the various parts of their personality as individual people coming together around a campfire in the woods, sitting on beach chairs at the ocean, or hiking up to a remote mountaintop. Some people select a favorite indoor meeting place such as a den with couches and a fireplace, a conference room with high-back leather chairs, or a quiet room in a retreat center that they love. Other times people select a setting that is unique to them. For example, one man whose passion was making wood furniture imagined a circular picnic table that he had made and each part of his personality was sitting around the table with a glass of wine. A high school basketball coach selected the locker room of his school and imagined that the different parts of his personality were players on the team. As I talk about this I say to my patient, "Notice if any particular setting is immediately coming into your mind. If not, something is sure to emerge after today's session. Trust whatever image shows up. The image of a gathering place will make the Council more concrete and will empower your experience."

I also tell patients that it is essential to remember that the persistent and various thoughts and feelings about their dilemma are coming from distinct parts of their personality; some are dominant in the patient's consciousness, others are present but have weak voices in the inner dialogue. Other parts may be dormant or submerged and need an invitation to join the conversation. They are underdeveloped and need to be nurtured.

To help make the Council image more concrete, I have the patient talk about the conflict again. As he is talking, I find a label for that particular part of the inner dialogue or personality. "So one member of your Council is the *Father* part of you. It's important for him to be a good father who takes care of the needs of his children. Who else is at the Council?" The patient talks further and I interrupt and say "That's the *Playful Boy* part of you that is tired of being so responsible and wants to have more fun in life. Who else is at the Council?" After the patient talks some more, I say again "That's the *Businessman* part of you who hates his job, but is grateful that he makes good money and can pay his share of the bills. Who else is at the gathering?" After listening some more I state, "That's the *Fearful* part of you that is terrified of change. Fear is usually a dominant member of everyone's Council. It's always important to acknowledge his presence even if it's hard to admit that you are afraid. Who else is at the Council?"

This initial process continues for a time until there are five or six distinct inner voices that have been acknowledged and named. Then I will say, "It's also important to leave one or two empty seats. These are for mystery guests. We don't know who they are yet, but they'll show up. They're always an important part of the Council and are needed for a good resolution. Usually the other voices in your head speak so loudly that these parts of your personality do not get a chance to be heard. By leaving the empty seats we are inviting them to be present and are honoring the importance of their contribution." As the Council continues, these spaces usually get filled. Sometimes they are subconscious or weaker voices in the inner landscape; at other times they are unconscious fantasy parts or dark or wounded parts. Sometimes there are undeveloped or underdeveloped aspects of the personality that need to be encouraged to speak in order for the issue to be resolved.

The final member of the Council is the *Wise Elder*. His or her presence at the Council represents a higher level of consciousness—the Higher Self—and serves a number of functions. It is the task of the Wise Elder to make certain that all the voices get heard and are respected, that certain voices are not allowed to dominate the conversation or attack the other members. The Wise Elder quiets down the judgmental voices with a tone of gentleness and compassion. He or she holds the large question before the Council, *What is in my best interest and in the best interests of the others involved in this situation?* The Wise Elder repeatedly returns to that question and encourages the members of the Council to tolerate the tension of unknowing until a resolution emerges that is "in the best interests of all." The Wise Elder's compassionate inner presence and the metaphorical image of a circular gathering (symbolizing wholeness) provide the container for all the new and powerful feelings that come up in the Council.

In the initial stages of the Council, I often will hold the position of Wise Elder until the patient recognizes and trusts that part of himself. Many people are not aware that they have their own source of inner wisdom. They are accustomed to relying on external sources (such as the therapist) to tell them what they should do. Others have not learned to value this aspect of their consciousness and therefore do not listen to its guidance. Oftentimes they will say with regret, "I should have listened to my gut (or intuition or inner voice)" about some earlier life decision. It is quite a challenge for us as the therapist to tolerate the tension among the parts of the patient's personality and not to align ourselves with one part that we think has the correct resolution to the situation. At times it is also difficult to be compassionate toward all the members of the Council, to trust that each has something important to contribute to a final resolution.

RICHARD

Richard, a priest in his early forties, was faced with a profound dilemma. He had just been offered a prestigious position in the hierarchy of the Catholic Church. He knew if he accepted the offer and did well, he would eventually become a bishop. This was something that he had fantasized about since his early years of training in Rome. In the past few years, however, Richard had found himself becoming increasingly attracted to several women parishioners. He was also envious of men who were fathers and wondered what it would be like to father a child of his own. The offer of this position put Richard at a crossroads moment. Indeed, for him it was a dark night of the soul.

Eight years earlier, Richard had been a member of a supervisory group that I had conducted for priests who were doing pastoral counseling. This prior connection provided a foundation of trust between us that allowed me to present the metaphor of the Council during our first session as a pathway of resolution for his crisis. He loved the concept and felt immediate relief that I would be able to guide him through this dilemma.

Richard imagined his Council convening at a mountaintop retreat center that he'd visited several times. One particular room that he really loved held a large stone fireplace. Facing the fireplace in a horseshoe arrangement, Richard imagined seven or eight very comfortable armchairs, each with a different part of himself sitting there. Over several sessions Richard and I dialogued with these distinct parts of his personality. Each had a lot to say about the situation he was facing.

The first to speak was the *Priest*. Richard described how much he enjoyed giving sermons, making accessible to parishioners complex aspects of Catholic theology. As a pastoral counselor, he liked the one-on-one engagement of helping people with their personal struggles. He loved the sacred moments of administering Communion and other sacraments. He felt quite confident that he was helping people and enjoyed his status in the community. Earlier in his priesthood, Richard had enjoyed being called Father Richard, but increasingly it saddened him. He felt a growing envy of men in his parish who had children and it was becoming harder and harder for him to suppress his yearning to have his own family. Because of the absence of his own father, as a young man Richard had grave doubts about his ability to be a good father. Over the years of working with kids, however, he had discovered a certain at-ease-ness in relating to them. We called this part of him *Rich the Father*.

As he revealed the next part of himself, Richard was more than a little embarrassed. This was the part of him that fantasized about making love to different women and enjoyed thinking that many women adored and desired him. "As a young boy," Richard explained, "I loved the swash-buckling movie hero who had great adventures and women swooning over him. I liked the way men admired him and women adored him." We named this part of him *Don Juan*.

Next came *Mr. Perfect*. This part of Richard embodied high moral standards and expectations of his accomplishments. Often he did not measure up to these expectations and *Mr. Perfect* could be relentless in his recriminations. This part was judgmental of *Don Juan's* lust-filled fantasies and hypercritical of *Rich the Father* considering leaving the priesthood to create a family.

The *Wanderer* was also present at the Council. Richard talked about his longing for total freedom, his desire not to be attached to anyone or any place. In fact, one of the things that he liked about the priesthood was that he could stay in a parish for just a few years and then move on. He also valued his freedom to travel to other parts of the country to give lectures on Catholic theology. The Wanderer dreaded the thought of being a family man and he thought of his own father as being trapped by the responsibilities of being a husband and father.

The final participant in the first gathering of the Council was the *Celibate*. Richard described a mixture of feelings about the vow of celibacy that he had taken almost twenty years prior. He spoke of the importance of maintaining the commitment to God that he had made in a sacred ceremony. Yet, as a theologian who had studied church history, he knew that one of the original reasons for the vow of celibacy was economic—to protect church property from being inherited by a wife and children. Toward the end of talking about the Celibate, Richard awkwardly and courageously revealed something else. The vow made him feel safe. He was quite anxious about his sexuality. Celibacy enabled him to avoid vulnerability and possible failure.

"So we've heard from six members of the Council—the *Priest, Rich the Father, Don Juan, The Wanderer, Mr. Perfect* and the *Celibate*," I summarized toward the end of the session. "For now I'll take on the role of the *Wise Elder* who holds the question *What is in your best interest in resolving this dilemma*? We'll convene the Council for a period of time until an answer becomes clear that is in the best interest of your entire personality. Between sessions allow the image of the Council to be in your consciousness and see what comes up. Also, imagine some extra seats as a welcoming invitation for mystery guests—some other parts of your personality—to show up."

Over several weeks two other parts of Richard's personality became important members of his inner dialogue. The first was *Little Richard*. Initially he appeared as a five-year-old sitting in the large armchair in the background with his head bowed and his feet dangling mid-air. As the Elder, I invited him to come in closer and speak. Little Richard talked about how scary this discussion was to him. Richard had first thought about becoming a priest when he was five. He recalled how excited his mother was when he first told her. She took him onto her lap, caressed him and said, "You are my special little boy." Little Richard related how this scene got replayed over the years and brought him frequent praise from his mother and other relatives. Little Richard was very worried about displeasing her and losing that special status. He worded it very simply, "If I leave the priesthood will people still love me?"

The *Builder* also showed up in Richard's imagery. Hammer in hand, with a tool belt around his waist and wearing a Carhartt jacket, he talked about how much he loved working with his hands, the pride he had in his carpentry skills. Periodically he helped his siblings with house repairs or building an addition. "Sometimes I fantasize about taking a sabbatical to volunteer for Habitat for Humanity or, even cooler, how great it would be to own a home where I could do whatever I wanted. It would be mine." Richard sighed deeply as he got more in touch with these feelings.

Father Dan also quickly emerged as the image of Richard's inner Wise Elder. In the early years of his priesthood he had known an older priest named Dan who was a father figure and mentor for Richard. For several years Richard was invited, along with a handful of others, for a two-week stay at a small farm in upstate New York that Father Dan had inherited. He remembered Dan as a kind, compassionate man who shared his personal struggles as a priest and encouraged Richard to find ways to express his individuality within an oftentimes oppressive church hierarchy. Periodically during a Council session I would interject a query, "So how would Father Dan respond at this moment? How would he be, what would he say?" Gradually the Father Dan image evolved into an embodiment of Richard's Higher Self, an inner source of nonjudgmental, wise counsel that held the big question, *What is in Richard's best interest at this time in his life?*

The Wise Elder

How the image of the Wise Elder presents is unique to each person. I encourage patients to find an image that fits with their worldview and personal narrative. For people in recovery from some addiction, I encourage them to consider the Elder as their own personal Higher Power. For patients familiar with Jungian concepts, I talk about their Self. For people from different religious or spiritual traditions, my patient and I seek an image consistent with that perspective. For some, the image of the Wise Elder is a family member or mentor who was a source of compassionate understanding and wisdom. "So what would your grandmother say right now?" I ask that patient. They carry the memory of that Elder with them and that person's guidance is available for them to draw upon. For those few patients who do not connect to any spiritual tradition or someone from their history, I ask if there is an author whose books they have read or some historical figure who represents a person of compassion and wisdom to them. Most patients are able to imagine someone who becomes a reliable image of the Wise

Elder for the Council gatherings. Some people, like Richard, are able to transform that image over time to represent more directly their own inner Elder.

The Council as a Container

Most people experience great difficulty in tolerating the amount of tension generated by the conflicting ideas and feelings that emerge in making big life decisions. It is almost impossible to contain for any length of time. Many people experience the tension among the parts of self energetically. They say, "I feel like I am ready to explode" or "I feel like I'm going to collapse." As they describe it, the energy is palpable. This is why so many people make a premature decision—it ends the tension. It is also why so many people use some addictive substance or activity during these periods of inner struggle to numb their anxiety.

The Council provides a metaphorical container for this tension and conveys the notion that it is possible for all the parts of a person to work together for the common good. It draws upon an ancient symbol of wholeness—the circle or mandala—to quiet the feelings of fragmentation and the fear of an emotional breakdown. By making the image of the Council very concrete—imagining a physical gathering place, giving vivid descriptions of the various Council participants, using language specific to such an undertaking of discernment—we assist the patient in bringing the process into a larger space, or container, outside their own head, reducing the holding of the tension in the body. By reminding the patient that "the Council members are gathered around the fire sitting on tree stumps" or "sitting in comfortable chairs in that wood-paneled room," the situation or dilemma is now "out here," in a container between therapist and patient, a more manageable, less overwhelming and frightening place for it to reside.

To help ease the inner tension between sessions, I suggest to my patients that they keep a journal exclusively for the Council. Each time before they begin to write I recommend that they re-imagine the place where the Council is gathering and envision each of the members sitting in their spots in the circle. Then I encourage them to write down whatever each member is saying on that day. The act of journaling serves to further concretize and empower the notion of the Council. It is another tool for taking the inner turmoil and placing it "out there." Patients usually report that the journaling reduces their physiological symptoms and helps them to feel that they are not carrying this conflict in their consciousness all the time.

We can also help to develop the container by the language we use. I find it very useful to encourage patients to substitute the word "and" for the word "but" when talking about their conflict. Commonly people will say "I feel this, but . . ." What follows is an opposing feeling or thought that negates, devalues or overrides what was just said. "But" encourages or increases tension. It places the feelings in competition with each other. The use of "and" encourages cooperation among the various parts. It helps to affirm the possibility that the various thoughts and feelings, no matter how different, can coexist. They do not have to compete against one another with one eventually winning.

Encouraging my patients to intentionally use the word *and* instead of *but,* or other negating words such as *however,* is important because of what it symbolizes. My therapeutic goal is to help patients to develop a more expansive and inclusive view of their inner landscape. Instead of experiencing their inner world as a place where there is ongoing internal warfare between conflicting parts of the personality, I want to foster the development of an inner atmosphere of coexistence where cooperation among the parts is possible. By my consistently—perhaps even annoy-ingly—interjecting the word *and* whenever my patients use *but* I am repeatedly conveying the message that it is essential that all the parts of the personality contribute to answering the question *what's in the best interest of the whole.* When discussing this I use the phrase, *honor our complexity* to describe the process of coming to a place of greater loving acceptance of who we are. Our culture does not help us to value the multiple parts of our personhood and teach us ways to get them to work together. So the Council provides an opportunity to do the job our culture fails to do.

Roots

Although it may not seem clear initially, each member of someone's Council has a history. It is essential to learn about their development to ascertain how deeply they are entrenched and what purpose they have served over a person's lifetime. This is true even for parts that seem universal (almost all Councils have a Critic at the gathering) or genetic (such as introversion or a "slow to warm up" temperament). They, too, have a history in how they have evolved with that person. One of the key roles of the therapist is to encourage, with gentleness and compassion, each of the parts to tell his or her story. In response, overly loud parts generally quiet down and more dormant parts develop a stronger voice. As a result, the purpose that each part serves becomes clearer.

At the third gathering of Richard's Council, I invited him to tell me more about the roots of Don Juan. A bright and articulate man, Richard rarely struggled for words. However, at this time he began to blush and became quite awkward in his speech, like an adolescent boy being asked to talk about his attraction to girls. This impression was confirmed by his story. Richard talked about his lust-filled teenage fantasies, secret cache of *Playboy* magazines and nighttime erections always accompanied by self-recriminations that "no good Catholic boy should have these thoughts," especially someone who wanted to be a priest. In the early years of his priesthood, Richard was haunted by sexual fantasies about attractive female parishioners who sought him out for pastoral counseling. One, in particular, he was very attracted to. He had encouraged her to come to his office for counseling sessions, partially to help her with conflicts with her son, but also, he admitted, as an excuse to see her.

At another session the Priest told more of his story. Because of his desire to be a priest, Richard had enjoyed a special status in his family and with the nuns in his elementary school. This feeling of specialness continued through adolescence and into his early twenties when he was selected to study for the priesthood in Rome—an honor reserved for seminarians who are considered to be future stars in the Church hierarchy. During that time, he often fantasized that in the future he would return to Rome as a bishop. Richard described the sense of pride and superiority that he felt in the early years of his priesthood. He believed fervently in the notion that the Catholic Church was the one true Church. He liked being part of a lineage that linked back to Jesus' apostles. He immersed himself in studying theology and considered that his task in preaching was to make Church doctrine understandable to his parishioners. And as he administered the sacraments, he would contemplate the long history of these sacred rituals.

In recent years, Richard had become disillusioned with the Church. He was enraged by its handling of the revelations of sexual abuse by priests and disgusted by its treatment of gays and lesbians. He frequently disagreed with the increasingly orthodox, conservative theological positions that were announced by the Vatican. Richard began to feel like a hypocrite on those mornings when he stood at the pulpit to preach. What he once loved so deeply had become contaminated.

Most people have some version of Mr. Perfect in their Council. It is that perfectionistic part of us that carries our self-expectations and is the internalization of parents', teachers' and peer criticisms that have occurred throughout our lifetime. Usually it shows up as a critical or judgmental voice. As we explored the roots of Richard's inner critical voice, it became clear that it was closely connected to the expectation that he was going to be a priest. He was held to a higher standard than either his brother or sister. In one of our sessions, Richard sighed deeply as he opened the door to some painful memories. Whenever he made some ordinary mistake as a young boy, his father or mother would look at him with disapproval saying, "You're interested in being a priest and you're doing that?" Richard started to cry as I said, "My heart goes out to that boy. How painful it must have been to hear that."

When he was nine, Richard recalled, he became enraged at his sister when she said, "You are not going to be a priest of God you are going to be a priest of the devil!" This tapped into his own fear of selling his soul to the devil. He remembered that he often imagined that the devil was on one of his shoulders and an angel on the other, each telling him what to do. When he failed to live up to his models of Jesus and the saints, he would rush to confession to ask forgiveness for his sins. As an adult man, this inner Good vs. Evil voice had become more nuanced, somewhat less black and white, but was still quick to judge him and make him feel like a hypocrite.

We explored extensively the roots of these various aspects of Richard's personality as his Council convened over several months. Periodically he would begin a session announcing that he had made a decision. This is a common experience in working with the Council. Because the tension among the members and the prolonged indecisiveness is hard to tolerate, often people will present a premature resolution. This is always a challenging moment for me. Part of me would like it to be over too. It is difficult to remain present in the face of this amount of tension and unknowing. I also feel compassion for the patient's struggle and aligned with their wanting it to be over. Yet much experience with this technique informs me that these early answers are usually premature and that we need to trust the process. At those moments I ask my own Higher Self for guidance and the strength to persevere. Then I take a few deep breaths to tap into my own well of compassion. Since this early decision usually comes from one or two parts that are dominating the inner dialogue at the moment, I gently ask what the other members of the Council think and feel about this resolution. In this way I am strengthening the metaphor of the Council as a container for the dynamic tension and uncertainty.

Mystery Guests

In each person's Council, inevitably there will be one or two parts of the personality that are not present in the initial presentation of the inner dialogue, but whose emergence will be essential to the unfolding resolution. By advising patients to leave one or two empty seats at the gathering, I am acknowledging their existence and importance. The idea of "holding a seat" is also a symbolic invitation for them to emerge and participate. As a therapist, I find it fascinating to witness the wide range of mystery guests that show up.

A pivotal moment in Richard's discernment process happened when Little Richard joined the Council. What was key for him was the awareness that this young boy part felt that Richard's only way of getting love was by being a priest. So Little Richard embodied his subconscious terror that if he left the priesthood people would no longer love him. By acknowledging his fear and exploring Little Richard's historical roots, Richard became more aware of the many aspects of himself, separate from his role as priest, that others found lovable.

In order to give a greater idea of the wide range of possibilities of mystery guests, I will offer examples from the Councils of two other patients. In the case of Paul, whose presence almost always seemed younger than his twenty-eight years, we convened a Council around the issue of finding meaningful work. He felt lost and clueless on his own. As soon as I mentioned the notion of a Council, however, he became excited about the image of the parts of himself gathered around a campfire deep in the woods. He felt hopeful for the first time in quite a while. After several weeks, Paul said that he didn't know whether or not one part of him should be in the Council. He called that aspect of himself *Innocence*. What Paul described was the part of him that saw the fun and joy in his life. He liked this aspect of himself and related how much he loved making other people feel lighter through his sense of playfulness and ability to have fun. However, he questioned whether Innocence should be at the Council because these discussions were serious and this part of him was childlike. As we talked further, it became clear that, to Paul, choosing a "lifework" meant growing up, entering adulthood, and leaving Innocence behind.

Paul's father was a practical, serious man who felt burdened by the responsibilities of providing for his family. Throughout Paul's adolescence and early twenties, his father had often lectured him about the importance of finding a job that paid the bills. Whenever Paul was playful, described his creative interests, or expressed some possible unusual pathway (such as starting a community-supported farm), his father would go into a long diatribe about the necessity of being practical. Paul would feel squashed. From these revelations it became clearer that Paul had internalized his father's worldview that becoming an adult with a career meant that all fun and joy ended. Meaningful work that one enjoyed and felt passionate about was not possible. By inviting Innocence into the Council and valuing him as one of the more important voices, a shift began to occur in Paul.

One day he asked me whether it was possible to be both innocent and mature. Was it possible that his father had it wrong? Could a man support himself and his family with meaningful work and still retain a sense of joyfulness and playfulness in the world? To Paul that's what Innocence meant—joyfulness and playfulness. I told Paul that I was able to do those things; my work is very serious and I am very passionate about it. At the same time, it is deeply joyful work that I love doing. I told him that playfulness is in my nature, too, and that there are often times when I bring that playfulness into my work. And I nurture that part of myself outside of work.

"In fact, Jeanne calls me Mr. Big O. when that lighthearted, laughing part of me that sees the bright side of everything is present. Even in dark times, that optimistic part of my nature comes through. Doing serious work and taking care of my family has not destroyed that part of me because I nurture it. You can nurture Innocence too—and have meaningful work." This session proved to be the pivotal moment in Paul's Council.

For Caroline, the mystery guest was *Death*. After a twenty-two-year marriage that had been good in many ways but that lacked an emotional depth she had always longed for, Caroline fell in love with someone else. After a year of having an affair, she developed a serious heart problem. Periodically her heart rhythms would become so irregular she would need to be hospitalized in order for her heart to be stabilized. She knew that the stress of her affair and her inability to make a decision about her marriage was contributing to her heart problems. The doctors had warned her that this condition could kill her.

Caroline had always loved to go for walks by the river. Her heart condition prevented her from walking very far, but still she would go and sit on a rock overlooking the river, imagining that her Council members were there with her. Although the ongoing dialogue was useful to her, eventually it became clear to me that someone was being excluded from the Council.

At our next session I said to Caroline, "You know that the situation with your heart has made you acutely aware of death lurking in the shadows. I think that it is time to bring Death into the Council. Her voice is important." Caroline nodded, "You're right. As soon as you said that I knew that I'd been avoiding letting Death speak. That makes the decision easy. If I only have a limited time, I want to spend that time with Alan. That choice has been harder for me to make. Maybe I've not been allowing Death its place so that I could just go on, not ever really making a decision."

Richard's Resolution

About six weeks into his Council, Richard began our session by saying that he had decided to accept the Church's offer of the prestigious position. It quickly became clear that the dominant voices in this decision were those of the Priest and Little Richard. "Being a priest is who I am. I have prepared my whole life for this. It is a big step toward the fulfillment of my dream," said the Priest. "Besides," said an agitated Little Richard, "everyone will be mad at me if I don't." After I polled the other members of the Council about his decision, I asked what Father Dan had to say. This was a decisive moment for Richard. He became quiet and reflected upon his memories of Father Dan. Then, as his right hand tapped his heart, he said softly, "Father Dan would say that being a priest is not who I am. There is more to me than the role of being a priest. He and others love me for just being Richard."

A month later, Richard walked into the office seeming as if a burden had been lifted. He talked about his walk along the ocean the day before. "As I walked, I found myself repeating the Bible passage, 'What doth it profit a man if he gains the whole world and loses his soul?' I knew then that I had to refuse the position. If I take it, I will be selling my soul for the power and prestige. I can't do it." He felt relieved and sad. The anguish of uncertainty was over. Though in many respects this was the harder decision for Richard to make, when he checked in with each of the different parts of himself he felt a sense of congruence, an absence of conflict. This inner state held as Richard made his preparations for this monumental life change. He would tell the bishop that he was under a lot of emotional stress and needed to take a leave of absence, giving him time to prepare for the next stage of his life. For now he felt the sadness about the ending of his dream to be a bishop. Deeper still, he needed to mourn the loss of the identity that had shaped most of his life.

Richard's Council had completed its work. He left the priesthood within the next year. The process of implementing his decision and the transition into an entirely new life became the focus of the next three years of my work with him. During that time he moved away from his Catholic religious practices toward a spiritual path that was more fit for this stage of his life. And while the Council no longer met in formal sessions, I encouraged Richard to deepen his relationship with his Higher Self. He would continue to "poll the Council" in preparation for our sessions and often invoked the image of his old mentor, Father Dan, sitting by himself in a corner of the small chapel he had built, dressed in jeans and a flannel shirt gently rubbing the bald spot on his head. He would smile warmly at this memory, with a mixture of nostalgia and affection for this man who had so lovingly encouraged Richard to be true to who he really is. Father Dan was just the right image of Richard's Higher Self.

Continuing to use the Council metaphor in an informal way helped Richard to take some decisive steps during his transition. He used his background of pastoral counseling to develop a psychotherapy practice as a way of supporting himself. The Priest part of him was grateful that Richard had found a way to continue one of his roles. Within two years he was in a relationship with a woman. They eventually moved in together and talked about starting a family. Richard was both terrified and excited. A new adventure was unfolding; a new life was taking shape.

MARIA

Sometimes it becomes necessary to reconvene a Council because a new major issue has entered a patient's life. In those instances the prior beneficial experience with the technique makes it much easier for my patients to become actively engaged in and trust how the process unfolds. Maria and I had used the Council earlier in her therapy and then her husband was diagnosed with cancer. This came as quite a shock to them. They had both been enjoying retirement and Vinny had been in good health for a long time. He had been having some persistent intestinal symptoms, however, prior to receiving the devastating diagnosis. After listening to Maria's feelings and expressing my compassion for them both, I suggested that it would be valuable for her to reconvene her Council to deal with this crisis. While I generally use this technique to work with a major life decision, Maria's story demonstrates how the Council also can be useful in a situation that is fraught with emotional complexity. For her, the Council became the container for holding the tension created by the differing feelings among the parts of her personality. It also provided an inner sanctuary for Maria to retreat to in order to better cope with the enormous emotional impact that this damn disease produced.

Whenever she was struggling emotionally, Maria would go to the ocean for sanctuary. So, as she had done earlier in her Council, she again decided that the parts of her personality would gather at the ocean. She imagined them sitting on blankets or beach chairs at a safe distance from where the waves were breaking. Sitting in the Council circle were: the *Frightened Little Girl*, the *Caretaker*, the *Wife*, the *Spiritual Seeker*, and the new, uninvited, guest—*Cancer*.

We spent the initial Council sessions allowing each of the members—each of the parts of Maria—to talk about how Vinny's cancer was impacting them. I would ask Maria, "Who wants to speak today? What part of you hasn't been able to share your feelings anyplace else?" Since Maria had become well acquainted with these various parts of herself through her other Council work, it was easy for her to connect quickly with the feeling state of each one. The first to show up was the Frightened Little Girl. She was easy to identify by the intensity of the anxiety Maria was experiencing. She was on the cusp of a panic attack much of the time. Maria knew that Vinny had been a good father to this frightened, young part of her, in contrast to her own angry and volatile father. A lot of old childhood memories had been activated as Maria anticipated the possible loss of the man who treated her with tenderness and made her feel safe in the world. She just wanted to stay under the covers in the morning and not get out of bed.

Another aspect of Maria's personality that had developed early in childhood was the Caretaker. She tried hard to soothe her mother's anxiety and cheer her up when she was cranky. She was the person her mother confided in about her father and his unpredictable moods. As an adult, Maria continued this Caretaker role with friends and colleagues as well as with Vinny. She had done a lot of intensive psychological work to change that pattern of putting her own needs aside to take care of the needs of others. With this newfound freedom, she had begun to really enjoy retirement with Vinny. Now he was sick and undergoing treatment. Maria was angry and resentful that just as she was beginning to focus on herself, the Caretaker was being forced out of retirement.

Maria and I had long conversations over the year of Vinny's treatment. She would often feel overwhelmed by the complexity of all she felt. She used a journal between sessions to help contain the swirl of emotions surrounding her. She did not want her fear and anger to get in the way of her taking care of Vinny. Writing about it helped. Using imagery in our sessions helped too. I remember one session, as Maria imagined the different parts of herself gathered at the water's edge, the Wife recalling all the times throughout their marriage that she and Vinny had enjoyed spending hours at the beach. She would wander along the shore collecting shells while he went body surfing. Maria cried, saying, "I never even considered that he might die before me. His father lived to be ninety-five and Vinny's always been so healthy. I'm the one who's always going to the doctor. I always thought I'd go first, that he would always be with me. It's really scary to think about being here without him."

Maria imagined herself as having two wise Elders—the first was the more psychologically and spiritually developed part of herself that had grown tremendously through several years of therapy. She asked if I would act as a second Wise Elder. We laughingly referred to me as a "consulting Elder." She knew that I, too, had had cancer four years before and she asked if I would be willing to share parts of my and Jeanne's experience. She wanted to be able to better understand what Vinny was going through and she wondered what it was like for Jeanne, as my wife, to witness the devastating effects of the cancer and chemo. I told Maria I would be glad to talk with her about our experiences whenever she felt it would be helpful. One of the benefits of a heart-centered approach to this work is the freedom to periodically step out of the role of professional and simply be an ordinary human being.

Maria said that it was hard for her, as Vinny's wife, to witness what the cancer had taken from him. She was accustomed to him, since his retirement, spending hours each day in his shop making furniture. Now he was tired so much of the time that if he spent a half hour in his woodshop it was a good day. The chemo, visits to doctors, tests, discussions of test results, and decisions about treatment all left Vinny depleted and depressed. Maria felt the same. "I know that Vinny is the one being treated for cancer, " Maria said to me one day, "but, actually, I feel that *we* have cancer because it has affected every aspect of both our lives."

It took time for the voice of the Spiritual Seeker to present itself in Maria's Council. She was angry with God. After all the tribulations that Maria had already endured in her life why was this happening to her now? She had tried so hard to be a good person—why had God given her this cross to bear? Why didn't He just take it away? After several sessions spent railing at God, the Spiritual Seeker quieted down. Maria realized that the source of these feelings was an image of God that she had held earlier in her life as the Omnipotent One who tests people and then rewards the good and punishes the bad. She had been a Catholic most of her life but no longer identified herself in that way and had rejected the notion of that God years ago. What had been evolving for her over many years was a personal relationship with Jesus. As she reconnected with this aspect of her spiritual life, her anger diminished and she was able to draw on the daily life of prayer that she had grown to love. What was helpful to the Spiritual Seeker was a simple prayer, *Jesus please walk with me and give me the strength that I need to deal with this cancer.*

Maria's Wise Elder also encouraged the Spiritual Seeker part of her to use tools she had learned years before in Overeaters Anonymous. Whenever she felt that the ordeal of dealing with Vinny's cancer would never end, she would say to herself, *One day at a time.* Whenever she projected into the future and imagined the emptiness of a life without Vinny she would remind herself to focus on this day, this moment, using the phrase *Stay in the day,* and saying to herself, *He's still alive—what can we do together today?*

The Wife talked further about how often she thought about Vinny dying. She felt so sad watching his obvious frustration when he couldn't do ordinary chores. Maria mentioned that she had not shared any of her feelings with Vinny because she did not want to further burden him. Yet she missed terribly the in-depth conversations that had become so commonplace for them. She asked me then whether Jeanne had talked with me about how she was feeling when I had my cancer. Without hesitation I said, "In the beginning Jeanne would go into the woods behind our home and weep. She would call her sisters and just burst into tears. I didn't know that was happening because she wasn't telling me. I learned about it later. In fact I am still just hearing for the first time about some feelings that she didn't tell me about then. After a while though, I knew that she was holding back and I asked her directly what was happening with her. She, too, was hesitant to talk more openly, not wanting to burden me. And at first it *was* hard for me to hear how this was affecting her. I felt like *I* was causing my beloved Jeanne all this pain. But we found as we struggled through this, that it was a relief to us to be able to share how this damn disease was attacking both of us. Jeanne listened to so much about what was happening with me, I was glad to have a way to be there for her. When she talked with me about her sadness and fears I told her how hard it was for me to hear, how I felt guilty to be causing her pain. I asked her to forgive me. It felt good for us to be so intimate and for me to be able to console her. It felt more like a part of our normal life. The cancer had already taken so much from us," I told

Maria, "it would have been terrible if it robbed us of our closeness." As I shared our story, I told Maria that Jeanne and I, too, came to understand that it was not just me who had cancer—*we* had cancer. Maria was so appreciative of this self-disclosure. The phrase *we had cancer* validated her inner experience.

Sharing my story gave Maria permission to talk to Vinny more about what she was feeling and brought them closer together. I encouraged her to talk with Vinny about her experience using the Council metaphor and to consider that the multiple parts of his personality likely were also having a wide range of emotional reactions to the cancer. She began to ask him more regularly about what different parts of him were thinking and feeling. Gradually they realized that, in the midst of their pain, something wonderful was happening. Because of the omnipresence of the Cancer, their love and appreciation for each other was deepening to a level they had never before experienced. They had become so profoundly grateful for the simple moments of life—having a cup of coffee, eating a simple meal without the side effects of chemo, watching a movie at home, going to the beach and walking hand-in-hand, all had become imbued with the grace of preciousness.

During the year of her Council, Maria experienced the devastation and uncertainty that goes along with a cancer diagnosis. She witnessed the debilitating effects of the chemo on Vinny's physical and psychic well-being. She felt the deep sadness of all that had been lost, the anticipatory anxiety and grief of Vinny dying and her fear of being left alone. At the same time, each of the different parts of Maria went through a transition. The two Wise Elders—the psychologically and spiritually developed part of Maria and myself as a "consultant Elder"—became the facilitators of much of what changed for her. Through our use of imagery, Maria's Wise Elder was able to provide an ongoing source of reassurance to both the Frightened Little Girl and the Caretaker parts of Maria. When they became anxious that they were returning to the emotional unpredictability and deprivation of childhood, the Wise Elders would remind them that Vinny was not like her unpredictable and needy mother, but was an emotionally developed man who temporarily needed Maria to take care of him. And while it didn't look like Vinny was going to die soon, even when he did, she would not be emotionally alone in the way she had been as a child.

As a Wife, Maria feared most the loss of her beloved partner and companion. They had come so far together through the years of their marriage. With the return of her prayer life through the Spiritual Seeker part of her self and the ongoing support of the Wise Elders, Maria came to an awareness that it was possible for her and Vinny to have a good life—even with Cancer as their constant companion.

Maria had no mystery guest in her Council, but an uninvited one— Cancer. It was in no hurry to leave their lives. Whatever Maria and Vinny did, wherever they went, Cancer was an ominous, large presence. And while the Council did not help her make any life-altering decisions, it did help Maria to gradually come to a place of acceptance of a *new normal*.

The life that she and Vinny had been having and the future they were expecting to have were forever changed. Their uninvited guest— Cancer—would always be present as long as Vinny was alive. During the year since they received the diagnosis they had learned that it was possible to have a different kind of full and rich life even with Cancer walking along with them.

RESOLUTION

The stories of Richard and Maria provide examples of two different types of resolutions to a Council. While at times I will use the image of the Council in consecutive sessions to work on a very specific life dilemma or crisis, as I have described in their stories, often the Council becomes an ongoing working metaphor that my patient and I continually return to as we move through the series of smaller decisions that emerge during in-depth psychotherapy. My patients also report that they periodically utilize what they have learned in their Council by having mini-Councils at home or at work. In those moments when they are experiencing some intra-psychic conflict, they feel more able to re-imagine those parts of their personality in dialogue, tolerating the tension among them until a resolution emerges. So even with smaller ordinary conflicts my patients feel that they now have a life tool that helps them externalize and contain the dynamic tension and develop some more respectful coexistence among their various parts.

The Council is a very visual way to return again and again to the question, *What is in my best interest (and the best interest of . . . my family, my relationship, etc.)?* It is also a very visceral way to connect or reconnect with the complexity of our emotional life and to develop more fully the human capacity to hold many disparate feelings and thoughts concurrently, as they are represented by the image of the Council members.

(5)

TOUCH

In my practice, opportunities for touch arise often. After a painful, tear-filled session a woman patient who is feeling very fragile stands in front of me and reaches out to grasp my hands before she leaves the office. She says she feels deeply grateful for my willingness to be a source of strength during her time of brokenness. Another patient has spent the session sobbing about the death of her mother. My intuition tells me she could really use a hug before she reenters the world. I know that she has no history of abuse and so would not likely be triggered by contact. Another patient with a history of homelessness was told by his father, "You're a loser. You'll never amount to anything." He has just opened his own business. I have been encouraging him and mentoring him to get to this moment. If he were one of my sons or a friend I would celebrate the moment with a spontaneous high-five. At the beginning or end of a session, many of my male patients extend their hand seeking out mine for a handshake. From many years of individual therapy, workshops and retreats for men, I know the importance of this simple, ordinary, multi-layered and deeply symbolic way that men use to make contact with each other. At the end of a painful first session talking about his wife's terminal cancer, a man asks, "Can I have a hug?"

What should I do with these opportunities for touch?

Touch is one of the most ordinary expressions of human loving-kindness. Yet for many professionals in the field of psychotherapy, gentle, nonromantic, nonsexual touch is out of the question. Of course we have legitimate concerns about the safety of our vulnerable patients—how will our touch affect them? There are also important cautions to be raised about therapists who have not done their own psychological work—are they using patients to satisfy their own unmet needs for affection and physical contact?

I am acutely aware that touching patients is a complex area in which patient and therapist could easily step into a transferential minefield. From that perspective it is easier to make a rule: *Thou shalt not touch patients*. From a heart-centered perspective, however, it is important for us to slog through this complexity so therapist and patient can have a freer exchange of giving and receiving this vital expression of human love.

At this time in my practice, I most often respond to opportunities such as those I have described by touching my patients, unless I know that it is not in their best interest. I grasp the outreaching hands of my fragile patient. I know that she is expressing her gratitude for my help during this time of emotional shakiness. I suspect, too, that she is reaching out to make physical contact with *my* strength so that she may borrow it for a while until her own strength returns. After asking her permission, I hug the woman who is grieving the loss of her mother. I am expressing my heartfelt support and imparting a deeper sense of being held during a time when she is feeling desolate and emotionally isolated. In a moment of mutual celebration, I "high-five" the man who has just started his own business. I am acknowledging in an affectionate and very male way all of the difficult psychological work that he has done to get to this moment of triumph. I shake the hand routinely offered by male patients at the end of a session. For men, a warm, firm, sincere handshake is an affirmation that genuine contact has occurred during our time and that we look forward to meeting each other again. I hug the man who is struggling to support his wife as he witnesses the devastating effects of her cancer. Our momentary embrace is a natural act of compassion and loving-kindness. All of these seemingly simple, ordinary acts are transformative. In these meaningful moments, our relationship shifts from therapist-patient to two ordinary people sharing the human journey. To remain professionally neutral by not touching in those situations is to miss an opportunity for a deeper human connection.

THERAPIST ISSUES

Inside the tent labeled "psychotherapists," we are a diverse group of people, each with our own unique ways of expressing love. It is essential that we respect that diversity and not say that certain ways of expressing love are superior to others. Since one of the key goals of therapy is helping patients to become more authentic, it is critical that we model authenticity by bringing our ways of expressing love into the therapeutic relationship. For me, affectionate touch is a primary way of expressing my love. Over the years, however, I have supervised therapists who have not felt comfortable touching or being touched; their primary ways of showing caring were through words or other actions. In addition to encouraging them to explore in their own therapy whether their discomfort with touching is because of some psychological conflict, I have also helped them to value their ways of expressing love. Each of us needs to know and value our unique ways of being a loving person.

For the sake of our patients, it is important for us to explore our own issues about touch. Sometimes, after a difficult session, a patient will say, "Can I have a hug?" or "Can you hold me?" I have heard many colleagues say that the way they handle that situation is to say, "Therapists are not supposed to touch." From my perspective, that response does our patients a disservice. It is a rejection of the normal human yearning for contact. If, knowing the person's history, we are concerned about what our touching will trigger, then it seems more authentic to talk about the reasons for our caution and thereby invite a dialogue. If, knowing ourselves, our not wanting to touch is because it is not a comfortable way for us to express love, it is important to tell that to the patient. That, too, invites an authentic dialogue that honors both the patient's reaching out and our unique ways of expressing love.

It is beyond the scope of this brief chapter to discuss every possible therapist issue around the area of touch. By relating my own struggles, however, I hope to encourage readers to explore which of their own issues might create therapeutic dilemmas.

Issues around touch, physicality and sexuality are charged for most of us. In fact, I don't know anyone who is completely comfortable in all of these areas. Most of us have wounds, small or large, that go back to our experiences as children, adolescents or young adults. It is only by our own working through of these earlier experiences that we are freed to become both loving human beings and professionals who touch patients only when it is in their best interest.

Coming from an Irish Catholic family, it is a given that I would grow up with lots of conflict around physicality, affectionate touch and sexuality. As I have talked about in other places, my father was at times a frightening, physically imposing man. I tried to stay out of his way. My mother, while gentle and warm-hearted, was inhibited in expressing physical affection. I, in contrast, was naturally affectionate. As a boy, I would sense my mother tighten up when I would touch her. Early on I became cautious in approaching her, experiencing her pulling back as a rejection of both my need for physical affection and my way of expressing love. Over time, this developed into an inner belief that there was something wrong with my desire to touch and be touched. *Does my mother think that I am too needy? Is she worried that I might become a momma's boy?* I rarely ever witnessed warm embraces between my parents. Perhaps my mother was trying to let me know that boys and men don't seek out physical affection. Of course since my mother never talked about it, these internal questions that arose in my boyhood mind were all speculations about what was going on within her. In the absence of any explanation that she offered, what these negative experiences between us imprinted upon me was a sense of shame about that part of myself that yearned for an affectionate exchange.

As a young boy and a teenager, I became the target of playground bullies. Subjected to regular pummelings, physicality became even more conflicted. I got my revenge on the basketball court, ruthlessly elbowing other players whenever the opportunity arose. In the playground subculture I never saw any warm physical contact between older men or other boys. Anyone who did that would have been labeled as a "faggot" and subjected to humiliation. As a result I quickly learned to suppress any impulses toward affectionate touch with other guys. As a student in an all-boys Catholic high school, I had no idea how to approach girls, felt anxious—as most adolescent boys do—about my sexual feelings and, by my senior year, was on track to become a priest. Surely that would allow me to avoid facing the inner conflicts around sexuality that were growing increasingly difficult for me. Fortunately for me and any future parishioners I might have had, I didn't feel worthy to be a priest and left the seminary after two years. Otherwise, I might have ended up like several of my patients who were priests—filled with unresolved, unconscious conflicts about physicality and sexuality—who acted out their issues with parishioners.

Eventually I began my studies to be a psychotherapist, married and started a family. The caution I experienced in approaching my mother for physical affection carried over into my marriage. My wife at that time was also highly conflicted about expressing physical warmth. Fortunately throughout my training and the early years of my work as a psychotherapist, I was in my own therapy and supervision with competent therapists who helped me work through my issues with physical touch and sexuality. This helped to improve my marriage and also enabled me, over time, to develop greater authenticity in my relationships with patients.

As a young psychotherapist, I followed the therapeutic rule: *Thou shalt not touch patients.* Given my conflicts in this area and the depth of my deprivation in physical affection, it was in my best interest and the best interest of my patients to follow this rule. I was aware that my needs were not being met and I was cautious about using my patients to meet those needs. In those early years, I still carried a lot of shame about my sexuality and my desire for physical affection. So even when I knew that my inclination to give someone a hug was heartfelt and not intended to meet my own needs, I projected onto my patients that they would reject my reaching out to them in this way. They would think there was something wrong with me. So I held back. It took quite a while to work through this deeply imbedded sense of shame and self-doubt.

Gradually these wounds healed, and my own needs for more affectionate touch were being met. I started to take small, incremental steps in offering consoling touch and physical affection to my patients. I knew that I was doing this for their sake and not to fulfill my needs. When I was uncertain whether they would be receptive, I would say, "I feel like you could use a hug; is that okay with you?" As patients responded positively, increasingly I knew that loving touch, when appropriate, was an important part of the healing that was occurring.

Explore your own issues around touch. If you have not done this, you risk unwittingly walking into a transferential minefield and causing harm to your patients. After you have worked on your own issues, when the opportunity to offer consoling touch or physical affection arises, the only question is, *Is touch going to serve the best interest of my patient at this time?*

PATIENT ISSUES

The primary question for patients, as I see it, is one of receptivity. How will our touch impact the patient? How will she or he receive our hug or high-five or hand on their shoulder? Not surprisingly, most people easily receive the contact as a simple act of caring from one human being to another. Occasionally a patient experiences some minor initial awkwardness because we are unaccustomed in our culture to professionals expressing their humanness in this way. Mostly that moment of hesitation is brief and the patients easily take in the warmth of the contact. They appreciate that I am a professional *and* a human being who is responding to their suffering. However, I never assume that it is okay to make physical contact. I get to know a patient's histories and I always ask first.

Alex, a likable man approaching forty, usually entered my office wearing a black leather jacket and carrying his motorcycle helmet. A few months into our work, after one tear-filled session about the loss of a job that he loved, I asked, "Is it ok if I give you a hug?" Alex replied bluntly, "I don't do hugs." He explained that, coming from a highly homophobic family and working-class subculture, hugging between men was taboo. If I were doing a lot of deep intrapsychic work with Alex, I would have pursued this further. However, Alex had made it clear to me that he was in therapy to work only on certain pressing issues in his life. He wasn't interested in deeper psychological issues. For him, a warm handshake before sessions was acceptable, but other affectionate contact between us was not a comfortable territory for him. In his year of therapy with me we had many warm verbal exchanges but I never again initiated any other physical contact. The definitive tone of his voice said, "This is who I am and I want you to respect that." So I did.

Monica was a highly anxious woman living in a marriage without affection or sexual contact for at least ten years. For the most part she and her husband had what, in an earlier era, would have been called a "marriage of convenience." As a child, Monica received very little affection from either of her parents. Clearly she was starving for some warm human contact. Earlier in my career, naïve about the potential reactions triggered by touch, I might have given her a hug, thinking that was what she most needed. However, one part of her story forewarned me about the danger of responding to that thought. A year before initiating therapy with me, Monica had had a brief affair with a man in her office. He, too, was in a loveless marriage. While their sexual relationship lasted only a few weeks, Monica almost needed to be hospitalized when it ended. The affectionate contact between them triggered the emotionally starved little girl in Monica, causing a regression to a dependent, infantile state. She felt panicky all the time, wanting to be with him every moment; she was unable to work or take care of ordinary household chores; she felt fragmented like "Humpty-Dumpty after falling from the wall." She ended the relationship, went on an antianxiety medication and eventually started therapy with me. When I heard Monica tell her story and understood the depths of her emotional neglect and deprivation, it raised a red flag for me: any kind of touch might reactivate that hungry little one and produce an unmanageable, dangerous regression. In the several years of our work, I never reached out physically to Monica, expressing my caring for her in other ways.

When Jennifer came to see me she was in a state of turmoil. About six months before, she had gone to her parish priest for pastoral counseling. After several meetings, Jennifer became aware that he was attracted to her. He would place his arm around her shoulder after their meetings and she would feel squeamish. She felt increasingly uncomfortable around him. Then one day he tried to kiss her. Embarrassed, annoyed and feeling guilty, she left and never returned. Jennifer spent the first months of her therapy with me dealing with her feelings about this experience. She felt guilty and disloyal to her husband that she had continued to meet with the priest even after she knew he was attracted to her. She was outraged that he had overstepped the boundary of their relationship, and she felt he had contaminated her spiritual relationship with God. Gradually, through our work, these feelings subsided and we began to talk more about the issue for which Jennifer had sought guidance from the priest in the first place: emotional and spiritual struggles about her physically handicapped son. Jennifer had almost died giving birth to Sam. When she spoke of her sadness about his profound limitations, I was often filled with a heartfelt desire to offer a consoling touch. But because of her experience with the priest, I held back. After a while I started to feel that my holding back was depriving her of this essential human connection. Finally, during a session when Jennifer was weeping about how painful it was to witness her son's frustrations about not being like other kids, I gently said, "I feel like giving you a hug, but because of your experience last year with your pastor, I'm feeling somewhat hesitant to do so. It is part of my nature to be affectionate and consoling in that way, but I've been holding back, not wanting to cause harm." Jennifer smiled and sighed, "I sure could use a hug right now. Believe me, I know that you're not like that priest. I can *feel* the difference in your intentions without your even saying anything. I feel safe with you."

At the beginning of our next session, I checked in with Jennifer to see if she had experienced any reactions to our hug the prior week. She smiled, "I know that you are a warm and affectionate person, and I could sense that you were holding yourself back in some way, but you don't need to do that with me. I appreciate very much that you are thoughtful and checked it out with me, *and* I'm so glad to have a hug." After that it became an ordinary thing for us to hug at the end of our sessions.

I have been seeing Sara for the past year. In that time we've had no physical contact. She comes from a violent household. Her father, a big man like myself, would frequently erupt with rage. He hit Sara, her mother and her two sisters. Her grandfather, too, was "creepy and nasty." Sara feels nauseous whenever she thinks of her grandfather's house. She has described several nightmares that are strongly suggestive of sexual abuse. While acknowledging this as a probability, Sara repeatedly tells me, "That terrifies me, I can't go there." Eventually, we may be able to explore that territory more fully.

Sara loves that I have tea in the waiting room and she always brings a cup into her sessions. She responds warmly to my welcoming "I'm glad to see you" when I greet her. She values my overt acknowledgements of her steps of growth and my handing her a tissue when she cries. Sara is easily able to receive these forms of love.

From my experience with patients who have been abused, it is often possible that, as the treatment unfolds, consoling touch can be part of the healing process. When a patient has worked through earlier trauma, an affectionate hug can transform something that was violent into something that is a soothing consolation. A response that was one of recoiling in self-protection can become an openness to tender human touch. These moments, when a patient learns that safe touch is possible, are tremendously healing moments, both physically and psychologically. It is my hope that Sara, too, will be able to accept a warm hug. I do know, however, that now is not the time.

Learning to read and respect the body language of our patients is a skill that all of us need to develop and fine tune as we grow in our ability as psychotherapists. My patient Dave would always move unusually far away from me as I held the door for him to enter the office. As he would get up to leave, he would pull his torso away in an awkward, leaning-backward motion. And while it is ordinary for me to shake hands with my male patients, Dave's body language told me that any kind of contact would have made him very uncomfortable.

Dave described himself as feeling "very different from other people." Initially, I thought that perhaps Dave had Asperger's syndrome or a schizoid personality. But the ways in which he described his relationship with his girlfriend, and the genuine emotional contact that occurred in our conversations, clued me in to some other probable roots of his awkwardness and disconnection. I suspected he had some very early, nonverbal wounds.

My suspicion was confirmed when Dave talked about the first years of his life. He was an unplanned child born to parents who were in a constant state of war. He was told that if it weren't for him, they would have divorced. Dave felt unloved, even hated, by his parents—an alien born into a world in which he didn't belong. These feelings were rein-forced throughout school for Dave, an awkward boy relentlessly bullied by the other kids.

After several months of good work together, I could sense a shift in Dave. He was less guarded, more relaxed. His physical awkwardness seemed to lessen. However, I remained cautious about offering any physical contact. Then one day, as Dave excitedly described a change in his usual pattern of behavior that represented a marker of clear growth for him, I said, "I feel like giving you a celebratory high-five; would that be okay with you?" Dave smiled and nodded his head. We joyfully high-fived, acknowledging his moment of personal triumph.

The ultimate goal for a heart-centered psychotherapist is to be a synthesis of a highly skilled professional and a loving human being. The capability to freely offer consoling touch and physical affection is a central facet of this approach. To achieve this we need to be liberated from the structures of absolute professional rules that state *Thou shalt not touch*.

We need to find a middle path. One cardinal aspect of being a professional is to do what is right for our patients. There are moments in every therapy wherein the most healing thing we can do is to offer heartfelt, consoling touch. Another core concept of being a healing professional is the dictum *Do no harm.* It is vital to know which patients would be harmed by our touching them. Likewise, we must be able to discern when the urge to touch comes from our own unmet personal needs. For the sake of our patients we need to be both freed from absolute codes of behavior and strive to develop a discerning wisdom that always holds the question, *What is in the best interests of my patient at this time?*

(6)

MEN

Men, more than women, need a heart-centered approach to psycho-therapy. I am aware that to say that may be controversial and overly simplistic. And yet, based on almost four decades of work with male patients and many years of leading workshops and retreats for men, I find there is more than a little truth in the notion.

When I first entered private practice most of my patients were women. Today, I work mainly with men. One reason for that has to do with the evolution of my work as a therapist and my own intention to focus on doing this work with men. In addition, changes in definitions of masculinity and femininity and shifts in gender roles have made men more open to exploring their emotional lives and their inner landscape. Thirty or forty years ago this was much less the case, except in highly educated and intellectual circles. My intention in advocating for a heart-centered approach in our work with men is to facilitate a greater level of comfort in the realm of the heart—a territory much more familiar to the women in their lives. I find three aspects of my approach to be particu-larly helpful with men: educating them about the language of the heart; using self-disclosure as a form of modeling; and using traditional male images such as the *warrior*, the *provider* and the *toolbox*, as a bridge to their emotional lives. While change clearly is occurring, it will take more than a generation or two to break down the ingrained male pattern of erecting barriers around their hearts.

TOM

Tom is a large, burly man with a powerful handshake. Seated across from me, filling up the chair, his presence gives the impression of oak-like steadiness—the epitome of masculine strength. Now sixty-five years old, Tom has consulted me because of the changes going on in his life. His wife, a psychotherapist, is about to retire and he is feeling anxious and inadequate. "She's always asking me how I feel—I hate that question. She's an expert communicator and I feel so . . . dumb. I'm usually clueless about my feelings. She wants to know how I *feel* about her re-tiring, how I *feel* about the changes that will produce in our life. I don't know *what* I feel or *how* to verbalize it!"

A former high school principal, Tom is now a well-respected con-sultant to schools. Like many men of his generation, he approaches emotional issues as problems-to-be-solved. One clue of that was how he announced in our first meeting that he would come for eight sessions. And, while this approach has worked well in his work life, Tom knows, intellectually at least, that his familiar strategies will not work for this "problem." Besides, his wife will not let him get away with his usual approach. He was clearly relieved when I told him early on that I have done a lot of work with men, that many men struggle with this issue, and that it is possible to develop the skills of communicating from the heart at any stage of life.

When Tom told me at our first session how much he hated the, "How do you feel about . . . ?" question, I simply nodded my head, smiled warmly and said, "You're not alone; a lot of men don't like when their wives or girlfriends ask that question." I elaborated that their inability to easily articulate their emotions feels humiliating to most men. They think the partner is being critical of them and sees them as inferior because they can't do this thing that is so ordinary to her. As a result, men often avoid conversations about their emotions to escape the pain of humiliation. In order not to trigger these reactions in my male pa-tients, I have learned to reframe the typical therapeutic question, "How do you feel?" Usually, I will ask, "What's happening in your heart right now?" when I sense that some emotion is being stirred up. With men like Tom, I have become especially attuned to nonverbal clues like a sigh or their hand touching their heart area as a signal to inquire about their emotions. In fact, whenever a male patient touches his heart, I interrupt the conversation and ask, "What about this is touching your heart?" or, "Something seems to be happening in your emotional heart at this moment. Can you give voice to what it is?" I interpret the gesture of touching their physical heart as a subconscious invitation for me to inquire into the realm of their emotional heart. Almost always at those moments, patients are receptive to my invitation to open up. They begin to be more attentive to what is occurring in their inner emotional life.

After a half dozen sessions, Tom reported, "I've been thinking about this a lot. I've always felt different from other men, like an outsider. I always felt that I was very sensitive, maybe too sensitive." He reported that his father and uncles were academics—they were his models of how to be a man. Their conversations were focused on intellectual concepts and finding solutions to problems. They rarely expressed any emotions except anger. He played football and basketball in high school and college. Most of his friends were athletes; his coaches, too, were traditional men. In order to be a competitive athlete it was important to disconnect from physical pain and emotional feelings of fear or vulnerability. In those worlds, in that generation, it was not safe to be sensitive and expose your inner life. He would have been ridiculed and ostracized.

As I was listening to Tom, I remembered my own trials in the project playground and a thought entered my mind, *Perhaps it's now a safer time for that sensitive part of you to come out of the closet.* However, before I could voice what I was thinking, Tom said, "This week I was remembering the moment ten years ago that my daughter revealed to my first wife and myself that she is a lesbian. I am pleased to be able to say that both of us were totally supportive of her. What is disturbing though, is the memory of what she shared at the time. She said she was terrified to tell us because she was anticipating our disapproval. I was deeply concerned then and still question this now. Why did she even question that I would love her enough to accept who she was? What had I failed to do with her and how had I not expressed my love enough that she would just know that it would be OK with me?"

Tom was very distressed at the idea that he had not clearly conveyed to his daughter how much he loved her. This revelation led us to explore how the life-long suppression of this sensitive part of himself may have affected his parenting. By following his models of what a man is supposed to be, he had learned to suppress his heartfelt emotions, to keep them in hiding even with the people he loved the most. Amidst the sadness that was palpably present in the space between us, Tom asked softly and with great earnestness, "What do I do about that now?" I told him about the thoughts I was having just before he related his daughter's story and continued, "Ten years ago your daughter came out of the closet, perhaps it's time now for your sensitive heart to come of the closet." Of course Tom asked, "How do I do that?"

Starting with that session and over the two-year course of our work, I encouraged Tom to use the language of his heart. Instead of wondering, *What am I going to do with the rest of my life?* I told him to rephrase the question and ask himself, *What is my heart's desire?* At another time, leaning toward him I said, "You have been a very responsible person most of your life. Instead of asking yourself what you *should* do in a particular situation, ask yourself, *What would make me more lighthearted?*" During another meeting, I suggested to Tom that whenever his psychotherapist wife asked the dreaded, "How do you feel?" question, he could take a few moments to gently tap his physical heart area as a reminder to connect to his emotional heart and respond from that place. "Of course you will feel very vulnerable—it will be both liberating and scary. Give yourself permission to be a beginner and do this a step at a time."

As our work progressed it was fascinating to witness how much more frequently Tom's right hand would lightly touch his heart while he was talking. At those moments I would gently ask, "What's happening in your heart right now?" In our initial sessions he seemed flummoxed by the question, but later on he would smile warmly, look at his right hand and talk about whatever was occurring. He told me how much he preferred that question to *How do you feel?*

As his therapy unfolded, intermittently Tom would remember some lines of poetry that were pertinent to our discussion. When I inquired further about his ability to recall poetic phrases Tom talked about his life long passion for poetry and the classics that he rarely revealed to anyone, especially not to other men. Yet poetic imagery, as he and I discussed, can be an excellent vehicle for expressing the language of the heart. My validation of this aspect of his personality acted as an invitation for Tom to tap more often into the well of poetry that he had memorized as a way of expressing what was in his own heart.

Tom awakened more fully to the awareness that he had probably been a heart person all of his life, yet most of the time had related to the world through his head. Since he and I have lived in the same era, we had many conversations about how masculinity was commonly measured in our generation, making it emotionally unsafe to expose our emotions. Because these patterns were deeply ingrained, it was hard to break through them. Yet Tom felt increasingly liberated as he experimented with opening himself to the heart realm. He became more comfortable in answering his wife's "how do you feel?" questions and their level of emotional intimacy deepened. Phone conversations with his daughter, who now lived in London with her partner, got freer and longer. Tom liked the fact that neither one of them wanted their phone time to end. As he moved away from being the critical, advice-giving father to being an open-hearted supportive listener, his strained relationship with his thirty-five year-old son slowly changed. Tom considered the probability that, much like himself, his sensitive son's heart was in hiding, protecting itself from direct questions about what he was doing with his life. Perhaps he needed to hear kinder words and a more compassionate tone from his father. As Tom was able to do this more frequently, his son began to ask, for the first time, that he and Tom spend time together. Tom was learning the language of the heart both in expressing his own emotions and in listening for clues when someone else was speaking from their heart.

GREG

Greg was a lanky, forty-two year-old graphic artist who entered the office with a graceful, loping stride as his ponytail bounced up and down. He had initiated therapy at the request of his wife, who had grown quite frustrated with Greg's inability to meet her needs for more personal intimacy. He, too, was concerned and perplexed by the anxiety he felt whenever Doris tried to get closer to him. It made no sense to him. He loved her and wanted to be close, yet he could feel his body tighten up at those close moments and he often had an urge to leave the room.

Greg recalled that his maternal grandmother, who lived upstairs in their small home in the suburbs of Boston, was the central figure in their family. She was a loud, opinionated, judgmental presence who demanded that the family cater to her. After several sessions of Greg describing how the family dynamics revolved around his grandmother, I told him that the image that came to me was of a Queen who sat on her imperial throne in their living room and demanded obedience from her subjects. As an artist Greg loved that image because it aptly captured the atmosphere of his childhood home. On the surface, Greg's mother appeared to be a strong, independent woman. As a sensitive, intuitive boy, however, Greg saw that his mother rarely went up against his grandmother and sensed that she was not really her own person, but rather a clone who was subservient to the Queen Mother.

Greg's father, a quiet passive man who spent a lot of time outside of the house in his work as an insurance agent, was the other core figure in creating a family atmosphere that contributed to Greg's issues with closeness. Even when he was home, Greg's father was emotionally unavailable, spending most of his time reading or watching baseball on TV. He, too, was a loyal subject to the Queen, fearful of her regal wrath. He rarely talked about himself or shared his opinions. Greg could not recall one instance of his father confronting his grandmother or standing up to her in any way. On the one hand, Greg was grateful that his father managed to keep peace in the family because for him to go against the Queen might have increased significantly the tension level of their home. On the other hand, Greg was angry and sad that his father failed to model for him how to openly express his own opinions and feelings. Moreover, his father's use of reading the daily newspaper and watching baseball as a refuge precluded any genuine closeness between the two of them.

Greg's grandmother, in her narcissistic self-absorption, created an atmosphere in which only her needs were important. She was not that smart, nor did she value the intellect or any form of artistic expression. Her court was not a safe place for a bright, artistic boy to express his needs or interests. As a mode of surviving, Greg submerged his inner life and became a submissive subject.

This situation was worsened by Greg's experiences at an all boys' Catholic high school. This Jesuit setting was primarily focused upon preparation for college. It was a fiercely competitive atmosphere, academically and athletically. As an adolescent with a sensitive, artistic temperament, Greg felt like an outsider and a target. It was not a safe place to express who he was. His main task again was to find a way to survive in this psychological war zone. Sometimes in these kinds of settings, a young man like Greg might find one teacher who befriends him or may witness some teacher who has similar sensibilities and can therefore become a mentor from a distance. Sadly, that was not in the cards for Greg. He felt emotionally adrift without any fitting male model either at home or in school.

For us as therapists, the whole topic of self-disclosure is a complex and controversial one about which much has been written. Should we talk about ourselves at all? And if we do, when do we do it? How much? How do we talk about ourselves with patients? How do we avoid contaminating our patient's therapy with our personal issues? Is sharing our story in the best interest of this patient? Each of these questions opens up an important part of the discussion. My own contribution to this larger conversation is to advocate for male therapists to share aspects of our personal stories and inner life, particularly with our male patients, in order to offer ourselves as an alternative model for a way of being a man. In my experience, one of the common threads in the narratives of my male patients is how little they know about the inner lives of their fathers. How infrequently their fathers expressed feelings, other than anger, that would reveal something of the depth of their emotions. As they struggle with their own feelings in therapy, these patients experience a hunger, usually at an unconscious level, for guidance about a different path that can lead to a richer inner life. From a heart-centered perspective, sharing ourselves is a very effective way to fulfill that need.

It is also essential for us to create a warm, welcoming atmosphere in which we are overtly open-hearted. This approach offers to our male patients an invitation to open *their* hearts and let suppressed parts of themselves be out in the world. Otherwise, what occurs is that our patients project onto our professional distance that we are like their fathers and many of the other male models that they have encountered. A golden opportunity, to offer patients like Greg a model of a man who has done a lot of deep, inner work and is willing to take the risk to share that, is lost. If I had taken that approach with Greg it would have left him adrift and he might even have stopped the therapy.

Early in our sessions, Greg talked about how anxious he was much of the time. Yet what others mostly saw was a calm exterior. After several sessions it became clear that underlying Greg's anxiety was a general sense that the world was not an emotionally safe place. My use of the word *safe* really resonated with him. Thereafter, whenever Greg described a state of anxiety I would reframe it by raising the question, "What is making you feel unsafe?" As the therapy progressed, it became increasingly clear to him that he was reacting with Doris and others as if he were still living with the Queen, or still in the Jesuit high school. These insights made rational sense to him and that was helpful, but Greg needed more. At a certain point, I decided to talk about some aspects of my own story that were similar to his and to share with him the things that had helped me to recover. Through this self-disclosure, I was offering myself as someone different from his father—a man who shares his own inner life and emotional struggles in an attempt to offer guidance. I explained to Greg that throughout my twenties and thirties, I, too, had a calm exterior that belied the anxiety I felt within. Then I said, "In my early forties, I learned to meditate and have had a regular practice since then. From this experience in meditation, I developed a kind of breathing technique that helped me to relax. Would you like me to teach you?" Greg was both surprised and pleased by my offer. He was not accustomed to this kind of male attention and guidance, and yet he was eager for it. "Can you teach me right now?" he asked. And so I did.

From that point on, Greg quickly developed a pattern in our sessions of stopping periodically for a few moments to breathe mindfully. Physically he would notice his breathing shift from being constricted to more expansive. It felt liberating to him. He also noted that, more and more at those times, he was able to connect to his emotions more easily and childhood memories were more readily available to him. In his everyday life, as Greg practiced the breathing technique for a few minutes a couple of times each day, he gradually felt his anxiety diminish. I also suggested that, when he felt himself distancing in response to Doris's efforts to be emotionally close, he gently tap his physical heart, take a few breaths and then respond to her. I added, "It's probably safer to open your heart to Doris than it was to express your feelings as a boy when your grandmother, the Queen, was in charge." Greg nodded in agreement.

Often when Greg was struggling with some issue, he would ask about my thoughts or what I would do in that situation. Initially, I got him to focus on why he needed to know what I would do. This led to discussions of his need for approval and being *other*-directed. What emerged, though, as the most salient reason for asking me these questions, was the absence, throughout his life, of a male mentor who could offer him guidance and with whom he could connect emotionally. Becoming aware of that lack of mentoring made him tearful. We talked about the deep sadness of that loss and the sense of emptiness he felt because of that void. Increasingly I realized that Greg's questions about my thoughts and what I would do were an expression of that lifelong hunger and that he was asking me to assume that role with him. With that awareness, I began to simply answer his questions and openly share more of myself. It seemed to me that to stay within the traditional professional role in response to his hunger for mentoring would only increase his sense of deprivation. To share myself in this way was an act of loving-kindness.

In a good mentoring relationship there is a "transmission" that occurs. By this I mean that the person being mentored takes in or internalizes the energy or the authentic presence of the mentor. Prior to the Industrial Revolution, fathers and sons spent their days together working alongside each other in the fields and shops and at home. In the past six or seven decades that has changed even more significantly—fathers no longer work near the home and when they are at home they are often exhausted from long days of work and commuting. They have little time or energy to be a real presence in their sons' lives. In preindustrial times, sons got to know their fathers by simply being with them. Of course I am not implying that in those days fathers and sons had some ideal positive relationship with deep conversations about their inner lives. Rather I am saying that through regular physical closeness sons had a greater sense of who their fathers were, at least in the outer world. Through that experience of being in each other's presence some "transmission" of how to be a man occurred. For many of our male patients, like Greg, that exchange never happened or happened in some minimal way. For a male therapist to be a genuine presence and allow his male patients to really get to know him is essential in mentoring the next generation of men. If we remain contained within a traditional professional role, not only do we potentially recreate the distant father-son relationship, but the opportunity for mentoring is either lost or occurs in a diminished way. At this stage in my career, I see this role of mentor as a primary and vital aspect of my ongoing work with men.

DOUG

My male patients in their twenties have grown up in the zeitgeist of an era in which men are encouraged to connect more with their inner lives. As a result they seem more receptive to psychotherapy and more readily responsive to my invitations to enter the realm of the heart. However, they have been raised with fathers, grandfathers and uncles from another era. They have been mentored by teachers and coaches who are also products of an earlier time. So, while there is greater cultural permission to define masculinity in a different way, they still have few models of what that actually means. One of the ways that I have found most helpful to bridge the gap is to use the metaphorical male language of earlier generations to teach my patients the skills that they are seeking now.

Doug is a lean, muscular twenty-nine-year-old who frequently rode his bicycle to our sessions. He would leave his helmet on the rocker in the waiting room before ambling into the office. In our first session he started out saying, "I'm here to find out what's going on with me. I have a good life, work that I like, two small sons and a wife that loves me. Yet, I am impatient with the boys, bicker with my wife, Alissa, and get these periodic down moods." Doug was clearly depressed. In the first few sessions, we began to understand why. As he became more engaged in being an emotionally involved father, Doug was becoming concurrently aware of what did not happen in his relationship with his own father. He was tearful as he talked about the contrast.

Doug's father was a plumber who built a successful business in updating the plumbing in older homes. He provided a good life for his wife and three children. Doug remembered him as a good man, well-respected in the community as a good neighbor who people could count on to be there when they needed help. At home, however, he fought a lot with Doug's older brother, bickered with his wife and spent a lot of time isolated in his woodshop making furniture for their house. Like many men of his generation, Doug's father lacked the interpersonal skills to engage on a deep emotional level with his wife and children.

As young men like Doug struggle to walk down a different path from their fathers, I find it helpful to use familiar male images to act as a bridge into the unfamiliar. "When your father reached into his emotional toolbox," I explained, "he found only two tools—advice-giving and the hammer of anger." Doug smiled. He liked the toolbox metaphor. As a computer trouble-shooter, he knew the importance of having the right tools. As we talked, Doug realized that he had more emotional tools than his father. However, he did not feel highly skilled in his use of these tools and was open to the possibility that there were others that he needed to acquire.

The toolbox metaphor made it easier for Doug to be open to my mentoring in the emotional realm. I encouraged him to further develop his ability to be a compassionate listener with Alissa. I emphasized the importance of softer voice tones and consoling touch to soothe his sons when they were upset. He was eagerly receptive to learning the technique of mindful breathing as a way of being more emotionally present with Alissa and the boys rather than being distracted by the many household chores that had to be done or the work problems he was still carrying in his consciousness. When Alissa was considering returning to work after being offered an exciting new position by her old supervisor, I presented to Doug the metaphorical tool of the Council as a pathway for Alissa and him to discern what was in her best interest and the best interest of their young family. I proposed that he utilize the toolbox metaphor when situations come up with Alissa and the boys. "Take a few moments," I suggested, "to imagine looking into your emotional toolbox and asking yourself, *Which tool would be most helpful at this time?*"

The word *provider* evokes a deep archetypal resonance for my male patients. Doug highly valued how hard his father had worked to provide his family with a good, middle class life with all its comforts and opportunities. Yet, he was becoming increasingly aware of what his father did not provide. He did not give Doug the consistent praise and encouragement he needed to develop good self-esteem. He did not offer soothing words or consoling touch to assuage Doug when he was upset. He did not offer himself as a guide to help think through the difficult problems of a young boy and adolescent. When I explained to Doug that most likely his father did not know that he needed those things from him or, that, if he was aware, he did not have the emotional skills to provide for those needs, Doug would nod his assent.

After several months of tear-filled sessions exploring what was missing in his childhood relationship with his own father, Doug came in and said that something important had occurred that week. He was outside watching his sons play and unexpectedly found himself internally vowing to them, "You can count on me. Whatever you need from me emotionally, I will provide for you." I felt quite moved hearing the depth of this moment of commitment to them, and praised Doug for this important emotional opening of his heart to his sons. The word *provider* had taken on a new dimension. He felt a powerful, almost primordial, inner resonance with this *felt sense* that providing for his children meant more than being the breadwinner; it meant bringing his emotional heart fully into his relationship with them. This was a big moment for Doug.

Another archetypal role of father is the *protector*. At the beginning of one session Doug talked about how recently his three-year-old son was coming into their bedroom at night crying about being afraid of monsters. Doug remembered that he never shared any of his fears with his father. He wanted to help Kevin, but wasn't sure how to console him and help him feel protected from the monsters. During this discussion Doug also shared how much he loved the few minutes each morning when Kevin would crawl onto his lap to snuggle while he was drinking his morning coffee before heading out to work. When I heard that story, I suggested to Doug that when he put Kevin to bed that night, he give him his own undershirt from that day with his smells on it saying, "I want you to sleep with my undershirt so that if you wake up you'll remember that Daddy is always here to protect you when you feel scared." Doug really liked that idea and so did Kevin. His nighttime fears gradually lessened.

As an elder, it has become increasingly important for me to take time out during sessions to acknowledge the courageous moments when my male patients open their hearts more fully. It is counter-cultural for these men to talk about their fears, to feel the spectrum of emotions that evoke tears and to expose their vulnerability. I tell them that they are being brave and courageous, not in ways that will win them medals or some other public acclaim, but in the realm of the heart. I feel that it is essential that I honor these moments when they are growing into being more *warriors of the heart*. Doug, like other male patients, liked my use of these traditional male words such as *brave, courageous* and *warrior* to praise him when he told stories of opening his heart. Initially Doug was taken aback by my atypical use of these words, unrelated to going into battle in wartime. Gradually, he realized that I was expanding or redefining what it meant to be a strong man. In the usual cultural definition, to cry, be vulnerable or admit that you were afraid would be considered weak. By calling him a *warrior* for his willingness to walk on the open-hearted path I was helping to value more the courage it took to go up against these common ways of measuring masculinity.

Much later in our work together, Doug asked me for guidance in helping his mother. For several months she had been experiencing a number of physical symptoms. After weeks of tests her doctors had determined that there was nothing physiologically wrong and prescribed a mild dose of antianxiety medication. From the beginning Doug sensed that he knew why she was having these symptoms, but he felt clueless about how to approach the subject with his mother. When I asked what he thought was happening, Doug told me the story of his Uncle Frank whom his mother both adored, because of his adventuresome spirit, and worried about, because of his drinking. Uncle Frank had come to live with Doug's parents two years before after losing his job. He was despondent because he couldn't find any work. One evening, about a year before Doug's mother's symptoms started, Frank got up from the dinner table, walked a few steps and collapsed. He was dead. Doug's mother never talked about this incident and rarely even mentioned her brother's name.

Using his new-found psychological knowledge, Doug felt that all the suppressed feelings about her brother's death were the cause of his mother's unexplained physical symptoms. "I still feel haunted by the images of Uncle Frank on the floor—it must have been much more traumatic for my mother. Yet, she never talks about it. Part of me feels compassionate toward her and another part of me wants to grab her shoulders and shake her out of her denial. Of course I know that wouldn't help. I want to talk to her about Uncle Frank's death, but I don't know what to say, I don't even know how to begin the conversation."

Doug and I first talked about his own feelings of losing his favorite uncle. Uncle Frank was a journalist who traveled the world. Some of Doug's fondest memories were of his spunky uncle coming to his home for the holidays and regaling the family with his tales of grand adventures. He wasn't even able to share those memories with his mother. As we talked about how he might broach this difficult subject with her, I returned to the metaphor of the toolbox. I validated his wisdom in not using a confrontational approach with his mother since she clearly was trying not to feel these powerful emotions. To "shake her out of her denial" would have been to use a hammer when the situation required a more subtle tool.

I explained to Doug that part of the compassionate path in relationships is that when we are going to talk about a difficult topic with someone we love, it is important to keep in mind who they are and to gently prepare them for what is to come. This approach will usually increase their receptivity so that they are more likely to listen to what we have to say. I reminded him about how he had learned when talking to Alissa, who had a history of a lot of criticism from her father, to preface his comments with, "What I am about to say is not intended to be critical of you." Doug nodded his head and recalled how that approach of preparing her had reduced Alissa's usual defensiveness and had enabled him to have some difficult conversations with less tension between them. I recommended to Doug that he prepare his mother by finding a way to convey in a gentle tone the message "Mom, I need to talk with you about something that is difficult for me to talk about. It is important that you know that I am coming from a place of love and concern for you." I suggested that he continue talking from his heart, even starting with his own feelings of loss and the trauma of seeing Uncle Frank die in front of them. With this reminder to Doug of the various emotional tools he now carries in his *toolbox*, he felt more ready to engage in this difficult conversation with his mother.

USE OF LANGUAGE

Initially when I use words like *toolbox, provider, protector* or *warrior* in ways that relate to the inner world of emotions rather than their more common use related to physical work or fighting or going into war, I get some quizzical looks from my male patients. Gradually they come to understand that I am expanding or redefining what it means to be a strong man. I am giving them a different measure to use that is more inner-directed that outer-focused. For me to use the language of *emotional courage, heart warrior, emotional provider* and *protector* provides a bridge from the familiar to the unfamiliar and helps them to value the strength and courage it takes to go up against the typical ways of measuring masculinity. My intention is to present myself as an elder of a different tribe who is initiating my male patients into a more heart-centered way of being in the world that is resonant with the kind of man they want to become.

FEMALE THERAPISTS

While this chapter has focused on the need for male therapists to consciously assume the role of mentor with their male patients, not all men see male therapists. In fact, many men who are entering therapy for the first time will specifically choose a female therapist—either consciously or unconsciously—because their relationship with their mother was significantly better than that with their father. A male therapist simply would not feel safe. Eventually, some of these men may go on to do some psychological work with a male therapist, but many of them will not. I hope that the ideas in this chapter are helpful also to women therapists in working with their male patients. While I do believe that the experience of mentoring for men *and* women is an important one, the ideas of a heart-centered approach to this work with men—helping them to learn the language of the heart, working through the emotional blocks that prevent them from being more open and receptive to expressions of love, encouraging them to focus less on problem solving and more on filling their *toolbox* with other emotional skills—can be put into practice by any therapist, male or female, who is interested in deepening their work with men.

⑦

LOVE BLOCKS

It was Sara's seventh session. The week before she had reported that she had discovered a lump in her breast. The mammogram was inconclusive and her physician was recommending further tests. In that earlier session she had decided to return to the cancer specialists in Chicago who had treated a prior episode of breast cancer four years before. "I trust them to take good care of me. They were compassionate and competent." She began this session by reporting her daughter's offer to take a week off and drive with her to Chicago. The night before our meeting, her husband had arrived home with airline tickets. Even though his new job was only a week old, he had persuaded his director that it was essential for him to accompany his wife for this evaluation. "I told both of them, 'Thanks, but I am going to do this by myself.'"

After a few moments, I said, "Those are two powerful acts of love that you are ready to reject." Sara nodded her head, sighed and replied, "I don't accept help easily. I have a steel door around my heart. It's like one of those doors that guard bank vaults and it's been closed for many years." I responded, " That's a pretty powerful image. I understand from my work with others over many years that you probably have some good psychological reasons for that degree of self-protectiveness. We are just beginning to get to know each other but I have some clues already about why that door around your heart exists. There are probably more that I don't know yet." Sara nodded, and seemed relieved that I was compassionate and not judgmental of her closed heart. Ordinarily I would have done some more exploration of her history, but I felt the pressure of time—she would be going to Chicago in ten days—and took a risk. "A few weeks ago you talked at length about your connection to the Native American path that you have been following for the past fifteen years. If a shaman were here, he would probably tell you that it is not a good idea to reject genuine acts of love. The Great Spirit does not like it when we reject love." Sara seemed to be able to accept that comment, saying, "That's true." Emboldened by her receptiveness, I went further, "Think about the impact on your daughter and husband if you reject their offer of love. How will it make them feel? If you can't accept their love for your own sake, can you accept it for their sakes?" Without any hesitation Sara responded, "That, I can do."

From my heart-centered approach, perhaps the most important goal of psychotherapy is to help people be freer in giving and receiving love. My particular focus is upon receptivity. It has been my experience that when we become more receptive to love, we naturally respond by becoming more giving. But the truth is, we all block love. Think of how often we struggle with simply taking in compliments, tighten up when someone becomes physically affectionate, have difficulty in receiving help when it is offered, become emotionally distant or start an argument when our partners become emotionally intimate. In all of these everyday instances, and many more, we are blocking love that is available to us. Of course it does not make any rational sense that we would ward off love. Yet, it does make emotional sense at some level of consciousness. There are usually some good reasons, understandable from the perspective of our personal stories, why we are unable to easily receive certain forms of love. I refer to these persistent, usually unconscious, patterns as *love blocks*. Twenty years ago, I coauthored a book with Mary Ellen Donovan entitled *Love Blocks: Breaking the Patterns That Undermine Relationships*. In this chapter, I am revisiting the notions described therein with the benefit of many years of additional experience in an increasingly heart-centered approach to my work.

There exists a natural human state of simply giving and receiving love. Watch infants and young children. Within the limits of temperament (some children are slow to warm up, others are introverted), some genetic difficulties (autism, Asperger's syndrome), and considering the developmental stage (infants are more receptive to others when in their mother's arms), generally young children take in and return love easily. By the time we are adults, however, most of us have experienced some degree of loss of that receptive self. Our therapeutic task is to uncover the reasons for that loss and to work through the blocks to receptivity. In that process, many of the primary transformative moments occur when the patient is able to take in the therapist's love.

I DON'T NEED ANYONE, I'M STRONG

Sara returned from Chicago with good news. The cancer had not returned and it was helpful that her husband was there to support her. As a cancer survivor, I know how relieved she was about this news. After sharing with her my relief, I said, "You learned something about the importance of letting people who love you, help you. You know how to be strong and survive. However, in order to have a rich life, I need to help you move from surviving to thriving. Part of thriving is being able to take in love in its many forms. We need to find out more about why it is hard for you to let others help you."

When she started treatment, Sara was unable to work because of her powerful depression. After several months of therapy, she announced that she had started to do volunteer work at an agency that helped women who had been abused. It was called The Survival Center. When she told me I just laughed and said, "If anyone is qualified to do that work, it is you. You can teach others how to survive." It was clear that Sara was a survivor and it became clearer why she had difficulty accepting help as she described her early childhood. Sara's father was an oppressive, rageful man who frequently exploded and hit whoever was in his presence. Her mother, an unforgiving, fearful, judgmental woman, was a religious zealot. The help that Sara needed as a little one—kindness, warmth, affection—was almost totally absent. What was offered to her—physical beatings and religious tenets that made her feel that anything pleasurable or fun was sinful—was abusive and toxic. From the age of five, she felt emotionally alone and often thought, *How do I get out of here? How do I get through this?* Like many people with the *I Don't Need Anyone, I'm Strong* love block, Sara had never really considered how her need to survive by her own strength impacted others. Given her history, this is certainly under-standable. As we worked with this she began to see how her declining their sincere offers of help would make her husband and daughter feel rejected. As she reflected on this lifetime pattern, Sara started to feel a deep sadness about the many lost moments in which she was depriving herself and others of opportunities for easily giving and receiving love.

While my approach as a therapist is always to provide a warm and welcoming environment and a nurturing and loving presence, with someone like Sara, who has experienced a lot of emotional neglect, I am more deliberate in my expressions of warmth and caring. I am providing for her a loving parent surrogate, willing to give emotional nourishment and guidance where her parents were unable. When the depth of her deprivation became clear after our first few sessions, I made a point of offering Sara some tea at the beginning of our next several sessions. She accepted and soon was making tea for herself. I am always sure to wel-come Sara with a greeting of, "I'm glad to see you again," something that she didn't feel from her mother and father. At the start of our work, Sara cried in every session. I would hand her a tissue, a small but intentional act of offering consolation. I would talk with her about difficult issues in a soothing, noncritical, nonintellectual tone. As she wrote in her journal of the insights that I offered, Sara said, "No one in my family ever talked to me in a way that helped me to understand what was happening." And I always acknowledged her steps in growth toward a different way of being in the world.

Within the heart-centered approach these conscious acts of creating an atmosphere of love in the office space and in our relationship are essential aspects of the healing. This helped to develop within Sara a sense of safety, trust and at-homeness. She reciprocated by becom-ing more open and receptive. With people like Sara, who grow up in a psychologically unsafe home, their psyches go into some internal hiding place and send forth their antennae to sense whether the outside envi-ronment is dangerous or toxic. If we remain professionally neutral, we invite the projective processes of these antennae to interpret our neu-trality as being like the parents. From the psychoanalytic perspective, this neutrality is desirable because, in that system, it is within the terrain of transference and countertransference that the healing occurs. From my experience with people like Sara that approach does not work. The patient remains shut down and self-protectively resistant. The therapy stagnates, takes forever or the patient leaves.

I DON'T DESERVE LOVE

One of the additional benefits of an openly loving therapeutic approach is that the patient's love blocks get exposed more quickly. After one of my comments praising the good work she was doing in therapy, Sara hesitantly commented, "It's hard for me to accept those kind words. I think inside, *If he really knew me, he wouldn't say that.*" As we explored this struggle in taking in my praise, it became clear that Sara's other love block was that she felt unworthy of being loved. "My parents really knew me," she told me. "When you get to know what I'm really like, then you won't think that I am such a good person." I replied, "So eventually I will get to know the real you, a bad person, a sinner." She simply nodded her head. This session evoked a couple of dreams in which the devil appeared. In talking about those dreams, Sara remembered how often the devil appeared in her dreams as a young girl. Laughter, silliness and fun were rare in her family. Sarah's mother, a religious fundamentalist, would call Sara a "little devil," or say to her, "God doesn't like it when you do such bad things." This pervasive attitude created within Sara, a core sense that she was bad and unlovable. Not only did her parents think that, but God did too.

As her story illustrates, Sara, like many patients, had more than one love block. This second one, *I Don't Deserve Love,* in my experience is the most insidious, undermining any efforts toward feeling loveable and loved. It is also one block on which the therapist's expressions of love can have an especially big impact. What Sara presented as "evidence" of her unloveability was that her parents, who knew her the best and the longest, found her to be unworthy of being loved. In slogging through this love block with her, my approach was three-pronged. The first was to discredit the source of her belief by questioning whether her parents ever really knew her. I suggested to Sara that her father's anger toward her had nothing to do with her personhood. He was chronically under-employed, felt totally powerless in his life and had been frequently abused by his own father. Sara, her siblings and her mother were simply the available targets on which to discharge his lifetime of rage. Her mother, battered by Sara's father for years, had become an emotional zombie by the time of Sara's birth. She sought solace in a fundamentalist sect that promised peace and joy in the afterlife. A central tenet of her religion was that all worldly pleasures were sinful and the renunciation of them earned a person a place in heaven. In order for her and her children to be "saved," Sara's mother needed to be hyper-vigilant. Normal childhood delights—laughing, singing and dancing—were all sins. Ordinary childish thoughts and feelings were "of the devil." As most children would, Sara internalized her mother's religiously motivated behavior as something personal about her. She felt unloveable to both her parents and God.

As her therapy progressed Sara began to talk more and more about how much she missed painting and other forms of creative, artistic expression. Her paints and art supplies were stored in her basement. She hadn't touched them in years and wondered if she would ever paint again. In addition to the feelings of sadness, what also became clear as she talked was a subtle sense of shame about her former passion for doing the artwork. In exploring the sources of this shame Sara remembered how much as a little girl she loved coloring with lots of different crayons and the freedom of painting with bright colors. Most of this she did in secret, because her mother said it was sinful to play in that way. It was acceptable if she colored within the lines of the religiously themed books that she got at church, but according to her mother, any form of free creative expression angered God. Of course, this made little Sara feel guilty about enjoying the art that gave her so much secret pleasure. And she felt confused. Her third grade teacher praised her artwork and said she had a gift for painting in this freely expressive way. As part of my ongoing efforts to discredit the sources of her belief system I said to Sara, "Something doesn't make sense to me. According to your religious beliefs all gifts come from the Creator. Your teacher said you were gifted in a unique way. So why would God give you a gift and then send you to hell for using it? That would make God a sadistic bastard. Do you think God is sadistic?" Sara smiled. She clearly liked that I was offering her a way to question the religious belief system that her parents had espoused. Perhaps, I suggested, some alternative image of a saner, more loving God could help her feel that a core part of her identity, her artistic self, was loveable.

The second prong of my approach with Sara was for me to be a deliberately loving human being toward her. As she revealed more and more of her inner life, I got to know Sara, the person. Rather than act in the role of the neutral professional, I made it clear to Sara that I really enjoyed her. My consistent encouragement, warmth, praise, welcoming attitude, celebration of her accomplishments, laughter at her jokes and other acts of caring, over time made her feel loveable. Not in a few days or weeks, but gradually, in small hesitant steps she was able to take in my love. Initially she responded by not believing that I genuinely felt this way. She said that I must have been acting in this caring manner because it was my job. But as she grieved the loss of having affectionate and loving parents, Sara was able to more easily take in my actions as genuine expressions of love.

The third prong of my work with Sara was self-forgiveness. From her parent's fundamentalist Christian perspective, Sara was a sinner—both as a child and an adult woman. She could easily recite to me a litany of her sins. Although she had long ago rejected all the bizarre beliefs of this sect, she still carried guilt that was contributing to her feeling of not being deserving of love.

At one afternoon session, Sara said that she had had a dream the night before in which she felt like she was being treated like a prostitute. She woke up in the middle of the night enraged. Even after a long walk in the woods that morning helped to dissipate some of the feeling, she still felt very angry. She told me the dream was triggered by a phone call from her daughter telling Sara that her ten-year-old granddaughter was going to do some modeling. This stirred old memories of what happened to her when her ex-husband had pushed her into being a model.

Sara looked away from me, saying, "I don't want to remember this, I don't want to talk about it." Gradually, with some gentle encouragement, she described what it felt like to be dressed in provocative clothing and to pose in whatever way the photographer wanted. She felt her body was not her own, it was being taken from her and sexually exploited to sell clothing. Sara remembered the humiliation and feeling like she was a depraved person. She knew that some of the other models were strippers and involved in pornography, and although she was not, Sara felt like the modeling was a kind of prostitution. During this time she began to drink more and to abuse drugs in order to numb herself to how soul killing this felt for her.

As she described this period of her life, Sara became more angry with her ex-husband for his oppressive coercion of her to be a model and for his sexual pleasure in watching this process. As his preoccupation with sex became obsessive, he started pushing for Sara to get involved with wife swapping and group sex. When his insistence became relentless, Sara filed for a divorce. As she told me more of the details of this chapter in her life, Sara became aware that a large part of her anger was with herself. How could she have allowed herself to be coerced into such a degrading position? Why did she think so little of herself that she allowed her body to be used in these ways? Over time we talked about how her parents' treating her like an object had contributed to her low self-esteem. We explored her conflicts around sexuality that were rooted in the extreme sexual repression in her home because of her mother's religious fanaticism. We also revisited her adolescent years when her father would leer at her in a sexual way whenever she got dressed up to go out. All of this helped Sara to come to a deeper understanding of how little sense of self she had at that time and how easily she could be coerced. She felt a much greater sense of compassion for that younger self.

As Sara's understanding and compassion grew, it made it possible for us to then talk about how the deep sense of shame and guilt she felt about that period of time was blocking her from being fully receptive now to the love that her husband Roy was offering. He was a kind, gentle man, yet Sara continually warded off his efforts at closeness and emotional support. While she was slowly able to let in more of Roy's love, it was clear to me that I needed to engage Sara in self-forgiveness work.

When I described to Sara my work with self-forgiveness, and how it evolved through my own personal process, she was both pleased and relieved. Knowing that I, too, had fallen and had found a way to lift the burden of guilt, gave her hope that she, too, could be freed. As I have already described in detail the self-forgiveness process that I use with patients, I will not go into further detail here about this aspect of the work with Sara except to say that the first image of forgiveness that came to Sara was of a very large heart. I like to think that my compassionate presence and simple acts of loving-kindness helped her to imagine that a big, forgiving heart really does exist.

I WANT LOVE BUT ONLY IF IT'S A CERTAIN WAY

Early in my personal psychoanalysis I went through an anxious period of feeling unloved. After several tear-filled sessions, my analyst gently asked me to consider a paradox: it was clear to him that there were a number of people in my life who loved me, yet I felt unloved. Why did I think that was so? I considered this and, after a prolonged silence, said, "Yes, they care about me, but nobody tells me how special I am. Nobody says that I am the most special person in their life." No sooner had I spoken, than an early childhood memory floated in: I was five or six years old sitting at the top of the stairs while the grownups partied downstairs. There was more than a little drinking going on. I overheard my father say, "Yeah, we weren't ready for a baby. Billy was a mistake." I started sobbing as the long repressed emotions of feeling unwanted gushed out of me.

Over a number of sessions we explored the unconscious wish underneath my feelings. I knew that my parents loved me, but they never made me feel that I was very special to them and that they were glad that I was born. I was still waiting for others to undo that early wound. I wanted them to tell me that I was the most special person in their life. Of course this was an infantile wish, and any form of love that did not carry that message did not penetrate. My analyst helped me to realize that my unconscious wish to be the *most* special was preventing me from being receptive to the love that *was* in my life.

As I released the emotions that had become imbedded in that repressed memory, I mourned the death of my wish for specialness. I began to have a deeper awareness of the complexities of my parents' lives at that time. In those days, couples didn't have the options for birth control that they have now. Besides that, my mother was a Catholic and I suspect that they never even had a conversation about birth control. Also, I was conceived at a time when they had serious financial struggles. I understood then that what my father really meant the night of the party was not that I was unloved or unwanted, but that I was unplanned. As I understood this, I felt compassion for the terror that they must have been facing, wondering how they would provide for this baby for whom they did not feel prepared.

My deepening awareness and compassion for both my parents and myself began to dissolve the block to receiving love that I had been up against for so long. I more consciously took in the love that my wife and family and friends—and yes, my parents—had been giving all along. Receiving that love, receiving the love that is available to me now, is what has helped me to heal that early wound. Working through my own block also helped me to be aware that, although the specifics of it may be different for each person, there is often some unfulfilled childhood wish underlying the search for a certain kind of love.

Reflecting back on the role of my therapist at the time, I am deeply grateful for his help in working through this unconscious block. However, as my own therapeutic approach has evolved, I can see how the constraints of theory and technique limited his more direct expressions of caring and appreciation for the uniqueness of my personhood. As I work with my patients on this and other love blocks, I know that my ability to provide these kinds of overt experiences of surrogate parenting—through consistent, loving presence, verbal appreciation of a person's unique qualities, direct affirmation that he or she is loveable—provides a necessary and solid path to healing these old and early wounds. I had hints from my therapist that he was fond of me. Yet it wasn't until years after my analysis ended, in his response to the publication of my first book, *Love Blocks*, that he more clearly revealed his feelings of affection. How much I would have benefited from knowing that during the course of my therapy.

While usually underneath this love block there is some unfulfilled childhood wish, *I want love but only if it is a certain way* is also related to a lack of understanding of the different ways in which people show love. Maggie, for example, is an energetic, idealistic, adventurous soul in a marriage to Todd that has gotten routine and stale. Maggie would love to fly off to Paris with her family. She wants Todd to plan the trip or even suggest it with enthusiasm. For her, that would feel like the ultimate act of love. She dreams about it a lot.

In Maggie's working class family there was no dreaming—only survival in the face of her mother's violent anger and her father's often suicidal depression. Her father did, however, hold one dream for Maggie, that she would go to college at Stanford University. The fulfillment of that dream provided her with a path very different from her parents.

Todd is not a man who would or could hold Maggie's dreams. He is steady and grounded but gets anxious even when Maggie insists on trying to get him to make plans for the family on the weekend. She becomes angry and resentful when he can't participate in a meaningful way and the whole family ends up having a meltdown. Maggie storms off to their room and goes to sleep, Todd feels like a failure and gets depressed and the kids spend the day bickering.

Maggie wants Todd to bring a sense of adventure to their lives. She wants him to have dreams for them. But that's who she is, not who Todd is. His way of showing love is by being the main caretaker and organizer of their home. He cooks meals, washes dishes, does laundry and vacuums. And while Maggie likes that he does these things and recognizes her own limitations in handling the household, she does not experience them as acts of love.

Maggie and I have talked a number of times about the different "languages" of love: some people express love through words, some people express it by giving gifts, some people show love through particular actions, etc. Maggie shows her love by getting the family energized and out into the world to do things. Todd shows his love by keeping a sense of order and cleanliness in their home. Neither is naturally good at what the other is good at. What might their relationship look like, how much more deeply loved would each of them feel, if they were able to genuinely receive love from the other in the way it is most naturally given? Invariably, after these conversations, Maggie looks wistfully out the window and says, "Yeah, but I *really* wish he would surprise me with a trip to Paris!"

Perhaps as we continue our work, Maggie will become more open to receiving Todd's love in the ways he is able to give it. She has certainly made it clear she doesn't want to end their marriage. And, perhaps if Todd comes to feel that his way of loving is being received, is acceptable—even good—he may be willing to learn a second language of loving.

LOVE IS NOT IN THE CARDS FOR ME

"I feel like a pariah. Everywhere I go I see couples and I'm always alone, always an outsider watching others enjoying themselves. I feel defective, like there is something definitely wrong with me and everyone knows it and nobody wants me around them. Even when I get my morning coffee I feel like the woman behind the counter is annoyed that she has to fill my travel mug."

Brian is forty-three and has had only one real girlfriend. Six months before starting therapy, this relationship of a year and a half ended without warning. A week after telling Brian for the first time how much she loved him, Tina dumped him. The most blissful and hopeful period of his life just ended. He was devastated and despondent. Tina and Brian were elementary school classmates and had reconnected shortly after her divorce. During their year and a half together, he felt like fate was finally shining down on him. Now he felt like he had somehow screwed it up and blown his only chance for happiness.

Early in his therapy Brian and I explored what had happened in his relationship with Tina. As the narrative unfolded, Brian remembered that numerous times Tina had talked about how much she hated men. Both her father and ex-husband were emotionally and physically abusive. She told Brian how different he was—kind, gentle and considerate of her feelings. He reported how, periodically, she would become distant, not want to see him for a week or two, not respond to his phone calls or e-mail. During these times Tina's explanation would be that she needed to focus intensively on work projects that demanded much of her time. However, I noted to Brian that there was a pattern to these periods of distancing; they frequently occurred after evenings of emotional and physical intimacy. I offered to Brian another possible explanation for what had happened, an alternative to his belief that Tina dropped him because he was a defective human being. "Perhaps your love frightened her," I suggested. "Tina was allowing herself to be vulnerable enough to love you. In her experience, all men hurt her. Perhaps at some level of consciousness, she felt that eventually you were going to turn out to be like all the other men she had known. Therefore, the smartest thing to do was to end the relationship before she let herself become more vulnerable." This hypothesis made good, rational sense to Brian. Of course it did not make *any* significant dent in his belief that there was something wrong with him. Brian's love block —*Love is not in the cards for me* because I am a defective human being—was deeply entrenched.

Our sessions, coupled with some conversations with his older brother, helped us to piece together how this belief system had developed. According to his brother, Brian's parents' verbal warfare had been going on for many years and had significantly worsened by the time he was born. While his father wanted another child, perhaps thinking that this would rescue the marriage, Brian's mother was angry that he even existed, trapping her further. She became increasingly self-absorbed and unresponsive to Brian's emotional needs. As most sensitive young children do, Brian interpreted his mother's inability to nurture him to mean, *there's something wrong with me.*

In school Brian was a scapegoat. He was intellectually superior to his classmates and, because he lived such an isolated life, had never learned basic social skills. There was one girl, however—Tina—something of an outcast herself, who befriended Brian. Excited about the relationship with Tina, one day after school, eight-year-old Brian told his mother about his girlfriend. His mother laughed and said, "Why would she like you?"

Because he had a rational, scientific mind, the intellectual insights about how his intra-psychic system had developed were quite helpful to Brian. His early childhood experiences helped to create an inner narrative that love was available to other people, but not to him because he was defective. Now in his forties, with no experiences in adult relationships except the profound disappointment with Tina, Brian was sure that the time for relationship for him had passed. If his mother didn't love him, what woman would?

After his many discussions with his brother, Brian decided to have a conversation with his mother. He knew better than to confront her at this stage of her life. Sixty-five years old and mourning the death of her second husband, she would only react defensively. This would create greater distance in their relationship and make him feel guilty. So Brian's intention was just to ask her generally about her life and see if he could learn anything that would be helpful to him. What stunned Brian was her revelation that his father had called her a "dumb hillbilly" throughout their marriage. Because our geographical area is in the foothills of the Berkshire mountains, the local towns are affectionately referred to as the "hilltowns." Brian's mother came from one of the poorer towns and his father repeatedly lorded it over her that he came from a middle class area. She felt a great deal of shame about this and would avoid going into town. She and Brian and his brother stayed close to home on an isolated back road. When she did have to go to town, she kept her head down to avoid the ridicule that she expected to receive.

This conversation made Brian more compassionate toward his mother and enraged toward his father. I told him that this was very important information that would help us to understand more fully why he felt so defective and like a pariah. I explained to him that in addition to the wounding things his mother had said to him over his lifetime, he was also carrying his mother's shame and that it had contaminated his sense of self. As a sensitive little boy, Brian had witnessed how his mother acted around other people and experienced how she carried that shame in her consciousness. I explained that *her* shame seeped inside of *him* and contributed to the feeling that there was something inferior and despicable about him. This resonated deeply for Brian.

Since it was clear that his parents, particularly his mother, did not welcome him into the world, my attitude at the beginning and ending of sessions was vital. For anyone who has serious issues of early emotional abandonment—and Brian did—times of coming together and parting are particularly important to be attentive to in therapy. I let Brian know that I was genuinely glad to see him and that I also looked forward to our next session. During one session I wrote on an index card, *You Deserve A Good Life*, and said to Brian, "Take this card home and put it some place where you will see it often. Then imagine that it is me saying those words to you. Imagine taking in those words with your in-breath and letting go of the feelings of defectiveness with your out-breath." I did not expect any instantaneous shift in his deeply embedded belief simply because I had given him this card. My hope was that, gradually, our evolving loving relationship would do the job his parents failed to do—to make Brian feel like a loveable human being who was entitled to some happiness.

In the middle of one Saturday morning session, Brian asked me if I would turn off the light alongside my chair. I reached over and shut it off. After a few moments of silence, I asked Brian what was happening emotionally for him. He hesitated and then said, "I'm surprised that you did that. I thought that you would be angry at my request. Who do I think I am asking for that?" We fell into a deep discussion about how he never expects anyone to be responsive to his needs, so he rarely even voices them. Because there is something wrong with him, his logic goes, he is not entitled to *any* form of loving-kindness, not even the simple act of turning off a light.

Several weeks later, just as I was beginning the session with my next patient, I noticed that Brian had left his coffee thermos on the table. I told the patient that I would return shortly, got up and, thermos in hand, went to the front door. Just as he was leaving the parking lot, Brian looked over and saw my outstretched hand holding his thermos. He parked the car, came to the door smiling and said, "Thanks!" For Brian, these simple gestures are significant. So, at our next session, I asked him what thoughts and feelings he had about the previous week's incident. As usual, he was surprised that I would go to the "trouble" to bring him his thermos. Then he asked me what I had thought and whether my other patient was mad that I delayed the session. "It wasn't any trouble," I told Brian. "I was glad to do it for you. I remembered you saying how much you like that particular thermos. I'm fond of you and so I didn't want you to have to wait a week to get it back." I also told him that my next patient wasn't mad at all, but simply recognized my gesture as a simple act of human kindness.

For many of us who were trained psychodynamically or were generally taught to maintain strict professional boundaries, Brian's leaving his thermos in the office creates a therapeutic dilemma. Do I simply leave it there until the following week? Do I call him and let him know it is there? Do I follow him out and return it? At an earlier time in my career, before I had the deep understanding I now have of the healing effect of loving action, I would have put the thermos aside and in my next session with Brian analyzed why he might have left it there. Did he not want to leave? Was he showing me that he trusted me by leaving his favorite thermos with me? At some point we may still look at those questions, but at that moment, because his ability to receive even small acts of kindness was so blocked by his deep feelings of defectiveness, the most important action I could take from both a clinical and human standpoint was to get up and reach out to him, thermos in hand.

Something broke through for Brian in that session. My simple, consistent and clear acts of caring and affection were beginning to break down his belief system. At our next meeting, he started by saying that he really wanted a relationship and knew that he had to make some changes in his thinking and behavior in order for that to happen. He acknowledged some small feeling of hopefulness and possibility and resolved to move away from his passive stance. Before we began to strategize about how he might do this, I reiterated to Brian the importance of changing his belief system. "You need to be mindful that, like myself, there are other people who are not reacting to you as if you are a defective human being. As you continue to deconstruct that old belief system, you'll be more receptive, not only to a possible life companion, but also to other kinds of loving relationships." *Love is not in the cards for me* had begun to break down for Brian.

At the beginning of one session Brian reported a dream that he remembered having had several times before. The central image was of a tree that was still alive, but with a scarred trunk and stunted in growth compared to other surrounding trees. He could see thick roots stretching far outward and deep into the ground. The roots were black and rotten with some toxins. It was clear to Brian that the tree represented his sense of self and that the infected thick roots were the childhood stuff that were preventing him from growing healthily into the person he could be. What was daunting for both of us was the cogent message of how thick, deep and far-spreading the roots were.

This dream offered an opportunity to talk to Brian about my notion of uprooting implants—how adults often carry inside of them something that existed in the atmosphere of their home that they took in as children as if it belonged to them. For Brian it was the toxic shame that his mother carried and his father's feeling of being trapped in marriage to an inferior person. By the time Brian was born their relationship had deteriorated significantly, and this sense of a rotting relationship was probably in the air of their home. Like any child would, Brian interpreted it as something defective within him. I told Brian that I wished I could surgically remove those contaminated roots and give him a nourishing, healthy root structure. He said that he would like to use a shotgun and just blow them away. We both became more resigned, however, that his therapy was going to be a difficult, arduous process. The good news in the dream was that the sun was shining. Brian interpreted this to be symbolic of a beginning feeling of optimism, reflecting some of the growth that was already occurring.

Brian loved to invent mechanical solutions to engineering problems. Since surgical removal of the root system was not possible and we couldn't "blow them away," I suggested that he could imagine some device that would metaphorically rid him of the unwanted toxic roots. I expected him to think of some kind of excavating machine. Instead, the next week Brian said he imagined creating a funnel into the root structure through which a pill would pass that would slowly get rid of the toxins. Each morning when he took the daily aspirin his physician had recommended for his heart, he closed his eyes and thought of the pill going through the imaginary funnel, penetrating deep into the roots. As he reported this, Brian smiled and shrugged. "I feel silly doing this," he said, "but it seems to be working. I feel less depressed." For this mechanical engineer to be open to the use of this kind of imagery says a lot about the therapeutic bond of trust that we had established and of his determination to remove this deeply rooted block to having more love in his life. Interestingly, over the next few months, Brian became actively involved in online dating.

OTHER LOVE BLOCKS

Although it is not possible to describe in one chapter all of the many different kinds of love blocks, I would like to sketch out a few others so that readers can get a deeper sense of the wide spectrum of ways in which we all block love.

For some patients, whenever someone tries to express love physically they pull away or tighten up. It's an automatic response that is not within their conscious control. For people with the *I Feel Threatened When Someone Gets Physically Close* block, any form of touch, however gently offered, makes them feel unsafe. Underneath this block is usually a history of physical or sexual abuse. Sometimes, however, at the root of this block is an absence of physical affection.

For other patients their expectation is that others should know what they need without them asking—*Why Can't You Read My Mind?* So if they express a need and their partner responds by fulfilling it, what they get is not real love or, somehow, what they receive is tainted or inferior to real love. Underlying this block is usually an unconscious wish to return to an infantile state in which the parent anticipates their every need.

For some others the feeling is, *Why Do I Always Have to Give So Much to Get So Little?* These patients often give the sense that they are keeping score in relationship. It is as if they have some inner ledger in which they are way ahead in the giving column and way behind in the getting column. They feel deprived and resentful. This block is usually rooted in a history of profound emotional neglect. The person tries to unconsciously communicate what their emotional needs are by being an emotional provider for others. They feel that others do not reciprocate and their inner emptiness intensifies.

RETURNING TO A STATE OF RECEPTIVITY

A paramount goal in heart-centered therapy is to help our patients return to a more natural state of receiving and giving love. What I have described in this chapter are three examples of blocking love that evolve initially from our patient's childhood experiences and then become reinforced by later events. For some patients this involves an inner view of themselves—*I don't deserve love.* For others it is a view of the world and their place in it that demonstrates what they expect out of life—*Love is not in the cards for me.* For others it is their view of other people and what they expect from them—*I want love, but only if it's a certain way.*

Our first therapeutic task is to unearth these often unconscious blocks. Then we need to explore with patients how these patterns of thwarting love originated and what has strengthened them. We acknowledge with compassion that for a long time these blocks have unconsciously served the function of trying to protect them from further pain. Now they are in the way of having a richer life, filled with the love they need. Our insights and skills in exposing these patterns are vital. However, it is our warm and compassionate presence and our other acts of loving-kindness that are essential in inviting the receptive self to come out of hiding. Our patients need to begin to trust that, if they allow themselves to be more open and receptive again, the outcome will be different this time. That process begins with our relationship with them.

(8)

SMALL HEART, BIG HEART

We all have small hearts and big hearts. Our *small hearts*, the emotional hearts of ordinary human consciousness, are profoundly limited. Because of the wounds and scars that we carry from our life experiences, our ordinary hearts have blockages in their capacity to be open and receptive to the amount of suffering that our work asks us to witness. Our small hearts are also limited in their ability to express compassion and loving-kindness with our patients. Moreover, we experience daily fluctuations in our capacity for empathy because of tiredness, toothaches, financial worries and other daily life issues. Our ability to be a loving presence also fluctuates with what our patients bring in each day. We can suddenly find ourselves in a transferential minefield in which our patient is projecting something onto us from her past or we are projecting something onto him from our story. Our work often places our ordinary emotional hearts in waters that are difficult to navigate.

At those times it can be very helpful to recall that we also have *big hearts* that are always present to assist us. I am using the phrase *big heart* as a simple way of naming an aspect of our personal higher consciousness. How you understand this notion depends on your cosmology.

Under the large umbrella of psychotherapists, we range from atheists and agnostics who use no spiritual perspective to inform their work, to those who feel that it is inappropriate to bring a spiritual perspective into the therapeutic relationship, to those of us for whom it is ordinary and integral to our ways of working. My challenge as a writer is to find accessible language to discuss the notion of *big heart* to this wide spectrum of psychotherapists.

I experience the same challenge in discussing this subject with my patients. In my current practice, I have as patients: an atheist, a secular humanist, a Buddhist meditation teacher, a Christian mystic, an energy healer and several other people who have no inclination toward discussing higher consciousness or interest in anything other than some practical help with their problems. I try to honor this diversity. Almost everyone in this wide spectrum can at least acknowledge that they periodically have experiences of a kind of love that transcends our everyday ways of loving. The momentary object of this deeper love may be a boyfriend or life partner, one of our children, our dog, our home, a dear friend, one of our patients or any one of a myriad of possible objects. Any attempts to use ordinary language to rationally explain these moments of extraordinary love are inevitably inadequate. This big experience of love, for however long it lasts, feels both light and large. It feels immediate, without any premeditation and, for a while, takes over our whole being. Afterwards, if someone were to ask us to explain why we feel that way, we might attempt to answer, but our response would always be insufficient. Or perhaps we might answer, wisely, that we cannot explain it, it simply *is*.

From my perspective, this extraordinary love emanates from our Higher Self. Someone else might call this personal higher consciousness their Higher Power, Buddha Nature or Christ Consciousness. There are many names for this ultimately unnameable aspect of our consciousness that transcends our everyday ways of experiencing. I think of my Higher Self as having a larger, more expansive, loving heart than the small heart of my ordinary consciousness. This big heart is capable of transcending the blocks and constrictions that limit my small heart.

Our challenge as psychotherapists is to find ways to engage this aspect of our consciousness while we are working with our patients. In attempting to do this, one of the core difficulties that we encounter is created by the human dilemma that we live at multiple levels of consciousness at the same time. How do we cut through the more dense layers so that we can access the lighter, less dense levels of higher consciousness when we need to? What I have found useful over time is to begin my workday in a way that allows me to clear out pragmatic concerns and set my intention to connect to this deeper level of consciousness.

Arriving at the office at least half an hour before my first patient is scheduled gives me time to prepare the space and myself for who will be arriving ready to do their work with me. I prepare hot water for tea and review my patient notes. About five or ten minutes before the beginning of my first session, I use a small wooden hammer to tap the antique Chinese bell that sits on the floor just inside the office door. This is a signal to remind myself that I am about to enter a psychological state that is different from the concerns of my everyday life. I use this time to open my connection to my Higher Self. To fulfill that intention, I have found it very beneficial to name that aspect of my consciousness and to develop an image of it. This enables me to have a more personal, heartfelt and concrete connection to an aspect of consciousness that would otherwise feel too abstract and ephemeral. I call my Higher Self *Wiseheart*. I think of Wiseheart as the pure essence of my uniqueness and the container of the compassion that I have developed from my own life experiences. I also think of Wiseheart as a carrier of the wisdom that I have received from my own therapists, teachers and other healing professionals that I have known. I consider Wiseheart a conduit for other sources of deep compassion and wisdom that are available to me through the collective unconscious. I visualize him as a bearded elder with a very large, warm heart and a kind, loving presence. Many years ago, my wife, Jeanne, gave me a piece of California redwood that had been carved into the wizened face of a bearded old man. I keep this carving in my office as an iconic image of my old friend, Wiseheart. In my prework period of preparation, I look at the carving and say, "Help me to be a vehicle of compassion and heart wisdom with my patients today." Then I take several deep breaths into my diaphragm and exhale through my mouth. I imagine myself breathing in Wiseheart's compassionate wisdom and breathing out the concerns and constrictions of my ordinary consciousness with the out-breath.

It is also possible for us to tap into sources of compassion and wisdom outside ourselves. On a personal level, these may be psychotherapists, teachers or other healing professionals who have been models for us and influenced us directly in our own healing process. We may feel a heart connection through the writings of someone like the Dalai Lama or Thich Nhat Hanh. Or, through the collective consciousness, we may connect to the wellspring of compassion and wisdom through the lives and teachings of historical figures. Depending on our beliefs, we can access any or all of these big hearts.

At this stage of my life, it is the lives and teachings of Jesus and Buddha that most influence me. To remind me of their compassionate and loving hearts, I keep a small statue of each in my office, out of view of my patients. In my preparation time I focus on them for a moment and, again, imagine taking in their loving energy with my in-breath and, with my out-breath, letting go of the concerns and limitations of my everyday consciousness. Then I open the door and welcome my first patient.

DURING SESSIONS

Once the work begins, we are in the psychological field of whatever each patient brings to us that day. Sometimes what they bring feels enormous and overwhelming: profound sadness or despair, terror or unrelenting anxiety, or, a huge void. When patients do experience these big feeling states, there is a palpable shift in the energy in the room. We can sense it entering our psychological field and disrupting our equilibrium.

In the field of these large feeling states it is understandable that our first response is often to shut down our hearts as a way of protecting ourselves from drowning in the onrushing tidal wave of emotion. We may not be conscious of this constriction of our small hearts, yet, we do notice some shifts in our normal way of being. We're checking the clock a lot. We're talking a lot more than usual or unable to find any words at all. Our minds are drifting off and we're having thoughts unrelated to the patient or any of a myriad of other responses. At other times it is something occurring in our own lives that makes it particularly difficult for us to be fully present. We are feeling miserable because we have a heavy chest cold. We had a big argument with our spouse or are preoccupied with the problems of one of our own children. Or we're worried about how we're going to pay that huge dental bill. Or our mother is dying. Under these circumstances, it is understandable that we wonder how can we get through the evening's work. How can we possibly be helpful to our patients when we're feeling like this? Our usual response is to try our best to slog through the work. These are moments when it is helpful to engage the bigger heart of our Higher Self.

I do this during sessions in the same way that I described earlier using meditational breathing and imagery. Only this time I imagine that I am releasing from my psychological field the feeling state of the patient that is intruding into my ability to be fully present. If it is my own feeling state that is getting in the way, I focus on releasing those concerns and depleting energies. Within a few minutes I feel an increased openheartedness and expansiveness in my thinking. I feel more fully present.

During these difficult sessions I often will imagine that the Higher Self of my patient is also present and available to be helpful. I will look above the head of my patient and quietly ask for their help in being open to whatever is possible. Depending on the patient, I might have them close their eyes and ask them to call on their Higher Self for assistance. Recently, in a very difficult session with a woman, I was asking her Higher Self to help her to be open when I noticed a change in her face—she had taken on the visage of an older woman. Curious, I asked her if there was some older woman in her life that might have something to add to our discussion. Almost immediately, an image came to her mind of a beloved aunt who was a great source of inspiration and a reliable loving support to her when she was younger. "If she were alive," she told me, "my aunt would be the person I would go to for advice and support during this time of transition. It's a comfort to me to imagine her presence and what she would say to me if she were here now."

ELLA

Ella, a hospice nurse in her late fifties, came into the office eager to share her recent experience. "I had an epiphany the other day," she told me. "My patient, Todd, is on a morphine pump. He told me he wants to be as aware as possible while he's dying. He knows he has spiritual work to do and he wants to be conscious for it. His wife, on the other hand, wants him to be knocked out. I didn't really understand why, until I found out the other day that Todd had been an abusive husband

and also had molested their son. My whole adult life I've just put these kinds of men who sexually abuse children in a category—they're just evil—even though Todd was also abused as a child."

"After I found all this out, I was sitting with Todd and he asked if I would rub his back. I'd done that for him in the past—I really believe in healing touch—but I wasn't sure if I could do it now, knowing what I knew. Todd was talking about his spiritual journey and his desire to remain conscious. I kept waiting to feel something in myself shut down to him. But it didn't happen! I rubbed his back and listened to him talk, and I kept feeling this openness. I just felt this deep sense of compassion for him. And it didn't go away. I felt like I was able to love the abuser."

I told Ella I felt a sense of joy for her in having such a profound experience with Todd. "It's no small thing to be in that place of compassion when your own feelings about what Todd has done are understandably so strong. In our last session we had been talking about how each of us have small hearts and big hearts. I remember how much you liked that notion. It sounds like you opened up into your big heart with him."

"There's more," Ella said. "I told you how angry I had been with my mother the week before, and how I had yelled at her for how neglectful she has been my whole life. Well, after this I went to see her and I had a similar experience with her—I like how you said I was in my big heart—I felt softer toward her; I felt a deepened sense of compassion. I guess I was in my big heart with her too."

By talking with our patients like Ella about the notion of *big heart* we are providing them with a frame of reference and accessible language to understand these transcendent moments in which they experience something extraordinary. As therapists we both validate and normalize these experiences by saying that we too have had them. We are thereby also encouraging our patients to be more open and receptive to these moments versus being fearful or dismissive of them. We help them to create an atmosphere for their big hearts to shine through more often.

TOM

For several sessions Tom—the burly oak-like patient that we met in the *Men* chapter—had been discussing with me his desire at this stage of life, as he struggled with issues of aging and mortality, to find some spiritual path that fit for him. Although he acknowledged that others benefited from traditional views of God and their involvement with faith-based religions, none of those approaches connected with Tom. They left him feeling empty and isolated from any authentic spiritual experience. Yet, throughout his life he had loved poetry and literature. He loved how these writers grappled with the larger questions of life. We called this aspect of his personality the Philosopher/Poet, a name that emerged during an earlier stage of his therapy when we were doing some Council work. During sessions Tom would often interject some lines of poetry or describe some literary character, valuing their explorations into the nonrational and meta-psychological realms of experience. It was intriguing to witness how our heart work had encouraged these somewhat dormant and secret aspects of his personality to emerge into a more prominent position.

One morning during this period of our work Tom announced in a discouraged and guilty tone, "I relapsed." That weekend he had had an eruption of anger toward his wife. Although he never hit anyone during his history of struggling with anger, because of his size his explosions were quite frightening to his wife. Toward the end of the session, after we discussed what triggered the anger, I presented him with an index card that said *Help Me To Forgive Myself* in order to help him deal with his deep disappointment in himself. Since we had done some self-forgiveness work earlier, Tom was familiar with the process. I suggested that he think of this prayer as being directed toward his Higher Self.

After this session Tom had lunch with an old friend who was a recovering alcoholic. Bob was familiar with the feelings of disappointment and shame that accompany a relapse. He encouraged Tom to develop a personal relationship with his Higher Power. Bob had struggled with the Christian language that permeates AA literature and did not believe in God or any deity as his Higher Power, so he could empathize with Tom's rejection of traditional religious beliefs. What he had found quite helpful, however, was to think of his Higher Power as some aspect of his own consciousness. This viewpoint had enabled Bob to develop an intimate relationship with his personal Higher Power. He suggested to Tom that he, too, begin to talk to that part of himself. This notion appealed to Tom.

I asked Tom to tell me about his personal Higher Power. In a warm tone and without any embarrassment Tom said, "His name is Jeremiah," as if introducing me to a close friend of his. He then told me about the two connections to the name. The first was to the biblical prophet. Tom spoke briefly of some of the tribulations that Jeremiah had undergone, but what was most compelling to him, was the theme of redemption in the biblical story. "More strongly, however, I think of Jeremiah as a mountain man, Jeremiah Johnson, the movie character Robert Redford portrayed. He was a strong man who was also warm-hearted." Recently Tom had started a new routine of using the early morning time before his wife awakened to sit quietly, to visualize Jeremiah and have a conversation with him. "I know it probably sounds crazy that I am talking to some inner mountain man called Jeremiah. Actually, I know it doesn't sound crazy to you, but it does seem crazy to that very rational part of me—but I don't care. It's a much better way to begin the day than sitting down to work at my computer. Besides, I like this guy Jeremiah." I reassured him that I didn't think that it was crazy and shared with him my own personal relationship with my Higher Self. "It's very difficult to have a relationship with an abstraction. So to name your Higher Self and visualize that part of you makes it more possible to develop a heart connection." Clearly this beginning relationship with his Higher Self had helped Tom to recover from the previous week's feeling of self-disappointment engendered by his relapse. As the weeks unfolded it also became evident that these ten-minute, early morning conversations with Jeremiah were becoming a kind of spiritual practice that fit for Tom.

Tom's evolving relationship with Jeremiah was his way of connecting to his *big heart*. With a warm smile and impish delight Tom revealed to me that periodically during the day he would check in with Jeremiah saying, "What do you think about this, big fella?" In the evening as he reflected upon the day, he would get a visual image of Jeremiah smiling with approval or looking with a quizzical, yet kind, expression as if to say, "Why did you do that?" As I listened to Tom's reports of these daily conversations it would always bring a smile to my face. It was clear that Tom's image of his Higher Power was not of some abstraction that lived in the heavens, but rather a dear friend who walked alongside him. As Tom's relationship with Jeremiah evolved, compassion for himself

increased and his loving acceptance of himself—with his limitations—
deepened.

BE GENTLE WITH YOURSELF

In almost four decades of private practice my second most frequently
repeated phrase—after some version of *How do you feel?*—has been,
Be gentle with yourself. I usually say this after a patient has been self-
critical or judgmental and as a prelude to some further comment or
question. Periodically I substitute the word *compassionate* or *kind* for
gentle.

A core goal of my heart-centered approach is to help my patients to
quiet down their critical internal voices and to develop a kinder and
more compassionate attitude toward themselves. From a traditional
psychodynamic perspective, I can conceptualize this aspect of our
therapeutic relationship as me being a loving parent surrogate to my
patients. In that frame of reference I am actively trying to undo the
harm caused by critical parents and other significant adults. My hope is
that by repeated exposure to me as a more loving person, my patients
will gradually internalize that gentler voice and begin to direct it toward
themselves. My experience bears this out. To further reinforce what I
do during sessions I write the phrase *Be Gentle With Yourself* on an
index card and have my patients carry this card with them or place it in
some prominent place as a reminder of me saying that to them.

I also think of my saying this phrase as an embodiment of a loving,
compassionate message from the *big heart* aspect of my patient's Higher
Self. Because the notion of the Higher Self is such an abstraction, it is
difficult for many patients to imagine what it might be like to have an
ongoing relationship with that part of their consciousness. In my philo-
sophical musings about who we are to our patients, I consider the possibility that a part of our role is to be a stand-in for the patient's Higher
Self. Through our frequent verbalizations of phrases of gentleness and
compassion, we become the voice of what their own Higher Self could
do for them. Gradually they become able to do it for themselves.

From this way of working, the big heart aspect of the Higher Self is
the ultimate personal source of our patients' self-love. For many of our

patients the concept of loving themselves is such an alien notion. Sometimes they equate self-love with narcissism. Often these are people who had a parent or other significant person who was selfish or self-absorbed and they are determined not to be like them. So the explanation that the source of the self-love is some aspect of their higher consciousness is more palatable, albeit unfamiliar. Other patients who have experienced a lot of judgmentalness or emotional neglect, which they have internalized, find it hard to imagine being nonjudgmental or nurturing toward themselves. For these patients the concept that their own Higher Self could be the origin of their self-love at least makes some sense. Yet they have no clue as to how that might occur. The first step in that process is for us to be gentle and compassionate toward them so that they have a feeling of what it could be like to be in a relationship with a loving presence. Then when we say *Be gentle with yourself* they have a model of a way to be. They can begin to talk to themselves in the way that we talk to them and imagine that it is their own Higher Self talking to them. As they have witnessed us being reliably loving for a long time they can consider the possibility that, within themselves, their own Higher Self can be a deep reservoir of dependable love.

BART

In his early twenties, depressed and emotionally adrift, Bart wandered the streets of a small New England city. He was homeless at the time and spent several years living in shelters. Bart vividly recalled the look of disdain evident in the faces of those who passed by him in the streets. He felt like a pariah. Now in his forties, struggling to support himself through odd jobs, he retains painful memories of their judgment. Because of these imprints, coupled with memories of a family that treated him like the ugly duckling—the son who didn't fit the family mold—Bart internalized their voices of judgment as his own. *You're a failure, a fuck-up. You'll always be a pariah.* This demeaning inner voice eventually undermines any positive feelings Bart might begin to have about current successes. It also ends up poisoning his relationships.

In working with Bart, I would often respond to his self-recriminations by saying, *Be gentle with yourself.* This helped to lessen some of the self-attack, but his internal judgmental voice remained virulent. I needed to find some way of further connecting Bart with his Higher Self. I pointed out to him that, in contrast to his lack of kindness toward himself, he often expressed great compassion when speaking of the suffering of others. At those moments, I told him, his connection with his *big heart* enabled him to rise above his own daily struggles and experience compassion for the pain of others. I encouraged Bart to direct some of this loving-kindness toward himself. Extending my right arm in front of me, I said to him, "Imagine that your hand holds your large heart, which can be so compassionate towards others. Then think of turning that heart toward yourself and allowing that gentle, loving energy to flow toward you. Imagine that love is seeping inside of you and penetrating the layers of negativity within you." Whenever Bart experienced these attacks from the judgmental part of himself he would describe the sensation of a knot tightening in his stomach. It was as if some aspect of himself went inward and formed this hard wall around itself as a self-protection against the barrage of criticism. When we did the exercise of turning his big heart toward himself, Bart would feel a loosening of the tightness. The progress with this was quite slow because the judgmental part was well entrenched and had been around for much of his life. Intermittently I needed to demonstrate the gesture of holding his heart in his hand and directing its loving energy toward himself both as a reminder and an encouragement to do it outside the office. During one session when we were doing this imagery work, Bart grinned impishly and said, "If I keep doing this, I won't need therapy anymore."

Bart has a passion for growing vegetables. Sometimes he fantasizes about having a small farm to provide organic food to his local community. I have encouraged him, when he is outside tending his garden, to take a few moments to imagine that the rays of sunlight are a kind of loving energy being directed toward himself. I ask Bart to imagine that these rays of warming love are passing through the multiple layers of negative feelings into the center of his being. I suggested that he do this for five or ten minutes at a time, using his in-breath to take in this love and his out-breath to let go of the self-judgment.

Sometimes when he does this exercise Bart considers that the source of this love is Spirit—his name for an external Higher Consciousness. Before beginning this series of exercises in his therapy, Bart had never thought of employing his spiritual belief system as a pathway for working with the judgmental parts of his own personality. His concept of Spirit had evolved as a synthesis of the Judaic beliefs of his family and the nature-based, somewhat pagan, traditions that he had explored as an adult. From the Jewish perspective, he saw Spirit as the loving aspect of Yahweh; from the pagan viewpoint, the symbol of the sun represented the nurturing love that is essential for all of creation. From his understanding of these spiritual teachings, this love was available in abundance and his task was to acknowledge his need for and become more open to receiving it. So Bart's moments of standing in the field and letting the sun's rays penetrate through the dense layers of negativity into some central, internal place, became a form of regular spiritual practice that fit for him. As an avid gardener and aspiring farmer he knew about the necessity of sunlight for his plants not only to survive, but also to grow into their fullest potential. So his spiritual concepts coalesced with what he was learning from gardening into using the rays of sunlight as the appropriate conduit for receiving love from a larger external source, Spirit.

Both of these techniques helped Bart to slowly develop a quiet warm inner place of loving himself. But through the process of using them he also became more acutely aware of the depth of his own self-criticalness. Through our work he was able to see that it was an amalgam of early judgments from his family, humiliating experiences in adolescence and the shame of being a homeless person. While the bigness of this made him feel a sense of sadness for himself and of being somewhat overwhelmed by a daunting task, the initial relief and peacefulness he felt from doing the exercises strengthened his resolve to practice the imagery more frequently so that a more sustaining change in the lifelong patterning could occur.

EXPANDING OUR SMALL HEARTS

As I reflect upon my evolution as a therapist, it is powerful to witness how much my own personal struggles and traumas have expanded my small heart, enabling me to be a more compassionate presence to my patients. From the beginning of my lifework as a therapist I think that

I have tried to be a source of compassion for my patients. And yet it is clear that each of the episodes of large struggle in my life have exponentially increased my capacity to be empathic with my patients going through their own life crises. I can feel a deeper connection to what they are experiencing and have an inner sense that I have more to offer them because of what I have experienced.

As therapists we all have these aspects of our personal journeys that uniquely prepare us to be more empathic with certain patients. In my life several stand out: the acknowledgement and working through of my father's alcoholism, two periods of despair and persistent suicidal ideation, initiating a divorce and the diagnosis and treatment of lymphoma. With each of these traumas my sharing of these parts of my life with patients, when appropriate, and in ways that fit for them at that moment in their therapy, deepened the emotional bond between us. Repeatedly my patients have said how helpful it was to them to know that I had gone through something difficult too. It gave them a sense that my heart was with them and also provided them with a beacon of hope.

My most recent experience of this kind was with cancer. When I got the diagnosis, I had been in private practice for thirty years. I had already witnessed the many times in my own work and in the work of other therapists that I've supervised, how our life experiences can expand our hearts. I had developed this way of thinking that, for us as therapists, *whatever increases our compassion is a good thing.* So I was not surprised that one morning as I was showering before going to one of my chemo treatments, this thought entered my consciousness—*The cancer is a gift; you are being prepared for what's up ahead. Your patients will benefit.* Of course some people will think that it is bizarre to even have a thought like that. Yet, in the context of what I have described, I think that it was my Higher Self presenting that notion. And how accurate it has been!

One clear example is Maria's story that I presented in the *Council* chapter. My description of what it was like to be a cancer patient and my sharing of what my wife Jeanne experienced as a witness to my illness, were very meaningful to her. It also has been beneficial to other patients who were diagnosed with major physical illnesses—diabetes, adrenal failure, chronic fatigue. Before I went through my diagnosis and treatment, I thought that I was caring and compassionate with those patients, and I probably was. However, I could feel how my own experience with illness had broadened my intellectual understanding of the psychological factors in serious illness and significantly deepened my compassion.

Shortly after moving in with his lover, Richard, the ex-priest discussed in the *Council* chapter, was diagnosed with diabetes. Initially when he received this news it felt like a death sentence. At our session the day after his doctor's visit Richard said, "I might as well be dead" and, "Just take me now" because of how he envisioned it would affect one of the great pleasures of his life, cooking and eating. He loved cooking for Rose and was looking forward to creating meals for her Sicilian family. Richard felt that the diabetes would rob him of these pleasures and was anticipating all the other losses of his familiar lifestyle that would occur. Prior to my having cancer I would have been compassionate, but I would not really have known how initially devastating it is to receive a life changing medical diagnosis. More than likely I would have unwittingly minimized the bigness of the impact. Now I could more fully say, "My heart goes out to you." Richard was aware that I was in recovery from cancer, but really did not know anything about what it felt like for me to cope with that disease. As I shared my experience with him, Richard heard more of the source of my compassionate responses and expressed his relief and gratitude that I would be a reliable ally in dealing with this disease.

My journey with cancer has also helped me to be a therapist who is more understanding and less afraid with my patients who are dealing with their own mortality. Because by the age of thirty I had had three experiences of almost dying by drowning, I thought that I was particularly attuned to that issue. However, cancer has taken me to another level of knowing. My lymphoma was very aggressive. A friend of mine, another psychologist in his early sixties, who was being treated for another form of lymphoma, died during the time I was getting chemo. That sent to me a very cogent message about what this disease could do. Although my recovery has gone well, I live with the possibility that the cancer could return at any time and this time it may take me. As a result, death is my daily companion and informs my decisions every day. With a deepened sense of awareness that my remaining time is limited and therefore precious, the question I ask is *What do I want to do with my time and who do I want to spend it with?*

One of my patients was struck by a car that suddenly pulled out of a mall parking lot while he was riding his motorcycle. He was catapulted thirty feet into the air and left with multiple body and head injuries. A friend who witnessed the crash said that he was amazed that Jack somehow crawled to the curb and then collapsed into unconsciousness. Afterwards the emergency medical personnel that responded to the accident reported that they thought he would die before they got him to the hospital. Jack consulted me after the accident to deal with the emotional trauma and the immense sadness of all the losses it produced. It also forced this very physically active and powerfully built man who told me that he had never experienced fear before, to confront the fact that he had almost died. When we entered that unfamiliar emotional terrain in his therapy, I told Jack about my experience with cancer and how it affected me. I said to him, "Those of us who have almost died are forced to look at something most men prefer not to acknowledge and certainly don't want to talk about." Jack was clearly moved by my sharing and wanted to know more of the details. That moment shifted something in our relationship. Thereafter, instead of greeting me with, "Hi, Doc," Jack would start our sessions with, "How are you doing, buddy?" and, as he was leaving the office, would say, "Take it easy, buddy." A bond of intimate connection was formed that carried us through the difficult work of his therapy.

One of the differences of having a therapy practice in a small town as compared to a practice in suburbia or a big city is that people have often seen me around town or we have had some informal conversation prior to their contacting me for treatment. Sean and I first met in the laundromat three weeks after his major auto accident. Sean was a passenger in an SUV being driven home after a Thanksgiving gathering by a friend who was drunk. She lost control of the vehicle; it flipped over several times and went down an embankment. His head smashed through the windshield. Bleeding profusely, he crawled out of the car and passed out. When he regained consciousness in the emergency room, the medics said they could not believe that he was still alive. Listening to his story while folding my laundry, I shared with Sean my experience with cancer. Thereafter whenever we would pass each other in town he would stop me and in a caring, but humorous way so typical of men, ask, "So how is the warranty holding out?" Knowing that it was his way of inquiring about my ongoing recovery, I would share with him my current physical and psychological status. Several months later Sean called me to ask if he could be a patient. Our therapy work focused upon the trauma of the accident and his never-before-discussed experiences in Vietnam. Sean told me that it was those in-town encounters that began to form the emotional empathic connection between us. Otherwise he would never have sought me out as a therapist. On a number of occasions he said that it was his awareness that I was still confronting my own mortality that enabled him to talk about the difficult feelings of almost dying in the accident and frequent confrontations with death in Vietnam. The genuine mutuality of our bond was evident in his pleasure in hearing my positive response to his intermittent inquiry, "So is the warranty still holding out?"

PATIENTS WE DON'T LIKE

Every therapist has experienced patients that he or she doesn't like. There are telltale signs. We become easily irritated or secretly judgmental with these people. We dread that patient's session and are relieved when they cancel. We hope they drop out of therapy. We find ourselves secretly agreeing with their partners and internally saying, "I would not want to live with this guy." It is a huge challenge to love this kind of patient when we don't like a particular part of them or, sometimes, their total way of being in the world. Traditionally, we are trained to examine what countertransferential feelings are being triggered by these patients. Is this person reminding us of some significant person in our lives toward whom we have unresolved feelings? Is this person reminding us of some part of ourselves we don't like or are unwilling to acknowledge? In my own practice I've often struggled with patients who always need to be right. They remind me of my father who always had to have the last word and had minimal tolerance for viewpoints that differed from his own. I have also struggled with patients who have a very narcissistic worldview in which they must always be the focal point—the universe revolves around them. Those patients triggered in me a disowned, or shadow, part of myself. In my own therapy, I had to acknowledge the repressed exhibitionistic part of myself and my secret desire to be seen as special by everyone in my life—wouldn't it be wonderful if the universe revolved around *me*! As I looked at the childhood roots of my reactions and worked through the feelings these patients evoked, I became more able to feel compassion, caring and even fondness for them.

With certain patients, however, this countertransference perspective is only partially helpful. Some people just seem to be unlikeable—it is hard to imagine anyone loving them. Erik was one of those patients.

A lieutenant of the correctional officers in the local jail, Erik was a tyrant who physically intimidated and psychologically abused his wife and stepchildren. He was the kind of person that would never have entered a psychologist's office voluntarily. Life, however, sometimes has a sense of humor. Six months before starting therapy, Erik had a stroke. After months of multiple therapies he had regained his speech and was able to walk with the assistance of a cane. However, Erik knew that he would never regain his previous physical strength or agility. He was unable to work in the jail and was forced to retire on a limited income. All the sources of physical, psychological and financial power with which he had once tyrannized others had been taken from him. The irony that this cold, cruel man was now the prisoner was not lost on his wife. She seized the opportunity and told him that if he didn't get into therapy she wouldn't take care of him.

Erik had a sadistic way of treating people. When his stepchildren had caused trouble for his wife he told them that if they didn't stop, he would push them off the roof. They stopped because they knew he was serious. He would share stories with me about how he had dealt with prisoners. He particularly had enjoyed the challenge of difficult inmates who would resist authority. He called them "frisky." One story that he shared in an early session really stands out in my memory.

One very aggressive prisoner kicked, spat at and punched some of the guards. They warned this inmate that he'd better not "fuck with the lieutenant." Of course, he didn't listen. With a dark glint in his eye and a sense of pride and triumph Erik reported, "It was the middle of winter, 5 degrees outside. I told three of the guards to strip him down naked and told another to open the window. Then I told them to close the door of his cell. I got the water hose, put it through the bars of the cell and hosed him down. After about ten minutes he was cowering in the corner. I told the guards to leave him alone until morning. After that he stopped being frisky." I looked Erik in the eyes and said, "You are a cold-hearted bastard." Erik just simply nodded his head and said, "You got that right, Doc."

How could I have compassion for Erik? From what source inside of me could I feel any kind of love for this sadistic, heartless man? Some of the strategies that might engender a therapist's compassion did not work with him. Imagining some history of childhood neglect or abuse, I inquired about his boyhood. Imagining some trauma from his stint in Vietnam, I asked some questions about his time there. He indicated clearly and consistently that he was unwilling to allow me to open doors into those parts of his story. While I was certain there must have been something there, I didn't know what it was.

This is a very challenging situation for us as therapists. How can we be a compassionate presence and show genuine loving-kindness towards patients like Erik or others whose personalities constantly trigger parts of our personal stories? Sometimes our own therapy can lessen the triggers, but still, we'll be affected. Some patients are so filled with darkness or their acts so heinous, that loving them is beyond what our small human heart is capable of.

I know that, for most therapists in private practice or in usual clinic settings, treating someone like Erik is an uncommon experience. We are more likely to see their victims. I have purposely selected his story for this chapter because he so tests the limits of our small hearts. What was effective for me in working with him will be even more beneficial in treating other patients who are less difficult to love.

With Erik, I first explored my own countertransference. It was helpful to acknowledge that I have a sadistic part of myself. As someone who views himself as a compassionate, kind person it is not easy to acknowledge this part of myself—I usually keep it behind a closed door inside of me, but periodically it comes out. What opens the door are bullies. I will notice it in my reaction to a patient's story in which he or she was bullied or abused or raped. The sadistic part of me wants to beat the hell out of the bully or perpetrator. I'll feel a surge of pleasure in the pummeling that I imagine administering. I know that I'm remembering my own experiences of being beaten by bullies. The sadistic part of me wants revenge. I was aware of these feelings as I listened to Erik tell the stories of his cruelties toward the prisoners and his family. The sadistic part of me wanted to beat the hell out of this sadistic bully—*he* was the perpetrator. My self-awareness prevented me from actually enacting some subtle, unconscious revenge towards him. It also helped engender some compassion for Erik to keep in mind that he likely had some similar childhood history that he was either unwilling to reveal or that was so repressed that it was inaccessible to him.

But what was most helpful in resolving the dilemma of how to love Erik enough to be helpful to him was to call upon *Wiseheart*. I needed to connect to the aspect of my Higher Self that contained a larger, more expansive, loving heart than the small, constricted heart of my everyday consciousness. Usually before each session with Erik, I would keep the office door closed for several minutes so that I could focus on the image of Wiseheart and do some deep breathing in order to create a psycho-spiritual space of receptivity. Looking at the carving of Wiseheart, I would softly say, "Help me to be of help to this cold-hearted man. Help me to be compassionate and kind. Help me to be an open-hearted, loving presence." I would not open the office door and enter the waiting room until I could begin to feel some shift in me. Whenever I would feel myself closing down during sessions with Erik, I would again look at Wiseheart and do my breathing.

One evening, as I reflected on our session that day, I recalled a tape recording that I had heard years before of a talk given by the spiritual teacher Ram Dass. His approach to this dilemma of loving difficult people was both whimsical and profound. He talked about each person having a physical form that we could see—short, fat, thin, homely, pretty. Each person also has certain characterological patterns, some of which are very likable, some of which are obnoxious, annoying or despicable. However, he said, underneath all of this is something we cannot see— their Soul, Higher Self, Higher Power or Buddha nature. Ram Dass suggested that we imagine privately saying to the deeper aspect of the other person, "Hello in there!" Imagine your Soul warmly greeting the Soul of the other, difficult, person with "Hello in there!" This memory made me smile. It gave me a way to respond to Erik with more ease. As he entered the office, I would imagine Wiseheart saying, "Hello in there!"

With Erik, I had to draw on all these resources in order not to hate him or become cold with him. I relied on my Higher Self to help me imagine that somewhere underneath his cruel, cold-hearted exterior, was a Soul trapped in a state of anguish, only waiting for death to release him. I imagined that his Soul had been imprisoned in its inner dungeon for a long time, held captive by the sadistic parts of Erik's personality.

My hope was that perhaps I could reduce the Soul's anguish by getting him to make some behavioral changes.

Because his illness had weakened him significantly, Erik was no longer physically intimidating to his wife, Donna. From his reports it became clear that Donna felt empowered to make demands on him, and, because she needed his income to pay the bills, she was willing to tolerate their status as roommates. Initially, Eric unsuccessfully tried to continue to assert his dominance over her with his psychological bullying. After several sessions of hearing his frustration and powerlessness, I said, with a mixture of compassion and enjoyment in the irony of the situation, "Because of your profound physical limitations, you are now your wife's prisoner. If you become a better inmate, she will go easier on you. If you are a 'frisky' prisoner, she will make your sentence a living hell. She will get her revenge for how you have treated her all these years." Gradually, he realized the truth of his situation and eventually stopped bullying Donna or trying to act as if he was still in charge.

After a year of coming to see me twice a month, Erik ended our therapy sessions. In that time, he never allowed me any real access to those aspects of his life story that would have helped me to understand what had happened to him to produce such a profound level of cruelty and coldness. Gradually though, he and Donna came to a negotiated truce. Erik knew it was in his best interest not to be a "frisky prisoner." He learned to treat Donna with more respect and appreciation. They continued to live in the same space while having separate lives.

At the end of the therapy, I was relieved that my work with Erik was over. I never grew to like him or his way of being in the world. However, I am grateful that my engagement with my Higher Self provided me with a pathway to be a loving human being with Erik—enough that he was able to make some incremental steps to becoming a better person.

Working with these images of *small heart* and *big heart* can bring us into greater connection with our deep, human capacity to tap into personal and transpersonal sources of compassion and loving-kindness. As we bring these qualities of love to our patients, we provide them with a pathway for a more peaceful coexistence among the various parts of themselves. Quieting the harsh judgments and self-criticalness that have been carried for a lifetime, we help them to bring their own big hearts not only to themselves, but also to their relationships in the outer world.

⑨

SANCTUARY

It is important for us to find ways to convey to our patients that we are a sanctuary for them. Through our loving, compassionate presence we are offering ourselves as a place of safety and refuge. Whatever struggles or suffering they are experiencing in the outer world, our patients need to feel that, once the office door closes, they are in a place of temporary retreat from that world where they can rely on us to be a source of nonjudgmental, loving-kindness. Even though they may not be able to articulate that they need this, at some level of consciousness, their wounded psyches are seeking that safe person, that place of refuge.

In Jewish and Christian traditions the *sanctuary* of the temple or church is an especially holy place. By intention it is sacred and inviolable, a place that has been reverentially dedicated to a holy purpose or person. During certain historical periods, the sanctuary was also considered to be a place of protection and asylum where a person could find immunity from legal authorities. It is from a metaphorical context that I am using the term *sanctuary* to describe an essential aspect of the therapeutic relationship.

Because so many of our patients come from families or other relationships that were psychologically unsafe or in some way violated their psychic space, it is especially important that we convey to them that their relationship with us will be different. By overtly expressing our loving concern and compassion for their suffering, we offer an invitation to their wounded psyche to come out and tell their story, that no harm will come to them. Indeed, the opposite is true—we will be kind and nurturing. This heart-centered stance contrasts with that of the neutral professional—the blank slate there for our patients' projections. When we offer ourselves and our space with the intention of providing sanctuary, the work with patients happens as they receive that message and respond, more readily revealing their stories and more receptive to our therapeutic insights and techniques.

To reiterate what I said earlier, I am not saying that all our patients need is love. Theories are important. Techniques are important. Competent clinical training and years of experience are essential. They, too, can convey a sense of safety to our patients. Over the years I have had a number of patients tell me that a previous therapist was a "nice, caring person" but had insufficient knowledge to help them. Good, solid knowledge and experience in our work and our continual development as compassionate and loving people is the synthesis needed to provide a sanctuary relationship for our patients. Then we can naturally be more openly welcoming, offer kind words and consolation, actively support and encourage our patients, work from an inner place of nonjudgmentalness and know when it is okay to provide affectionate touch.

Another facet of the notion of the therapeutical relationship as sanctuary is our invitation to our patients to become more whole. Because so many people come to us in a state of fragmentation or brokenness, most of them have some parts of their personality that are disowned or hated or severely judged. When our patients receive from us the message that the therapeutic relationship is a safe place to acknowledge and get to know those parts of themselves in an atmosphere of loving-kindness and nonjudgment, we are offering a gentle invitation for them to come out. As the therapy unfolds we are modeling a way of being that our patients gradually can internalize. The goal is wholeness, not in the sense of a static state of a solid whole, but more coming to a place of acknowledging all of the diverse parts of their personality, developing a sense of loving compassion—not always liking—for these parts and getting them to work together for the greater good of the whole person.

WELCOMING

Our welcoming presence and the warmth of our office space becomes a metaphorical container for this process. When I meet a patient for the first time I always greet them by saying, "Welcome." At follow up sessions, I take care to convey the message that I am glad to see them again. This attitude of openness and receptivity is intended to counteract the common experience many patients have had of not being welcomed into new relationships. For a number of them, their initial entry into the world was not an experience of being welcomed. Perhaps they had parents who did not want them or were in a state of depletion or depression; parents who were overwhelmed, in a fear-driven, survival mode without the energy or consciousness to show their child that they, as parents, were glad they were born. Other patients have had the experience of trying to join childhood or adolescent peer groups and being treated with indifference, rejection or humiliation. Many carry the negative memories of being summoned to the offices of teachers, school principals, coaches or priests to receive criticism. These experiences have left scars at many levels of consciousness and contribute to the sense of trepidation and anxiety with which a patient initially enters our treatment space. In order to convey the message that something different will happen in our relationship, that this is a safe place to be, it is important to make them feel welcome. If we say nothing in the first moments of our meeting or are neutral in what we convey, we are inviting our patients to project onto us from their previous experiences. Of course patients will project anyway. What a welcoming attitude provides is the possibility that, at some level of consciousness our patients will begin to feel that perhaps something different can happen here.

So much of what we communicate to our patients is transmitted nonverbally and at non-rational levels of consciousness. It is then important for us to ask ourselves: *Does my office space communicate to patients that they are entering a safe space in which they will be received with warmth, kindness and dignity?* Of course, as practitioners, how each of us creates that atmosphere will be unique, fitted to our individual personalities and the limitations of the physical space. However, it never ceases to amaze me how little thought so many healing practitioners give to the ambience of their space. I have been to see many doctors, chiropractors, psychotherapists and acupuncturists over the years whose space feels neither warm nor soothing. On the contrary, it is so often cold and impersonal. The lighting is harsh, the furniture uncomfortable, the artwork neutral and there are few personal objects reflecting the personality of the person. We've all become accustomed to this kind of sterile and impersonal "professional" space and, yet, for myself, it is incongruent with what is supposed to happen there—healing our bodies and our psyches. Freud and Jung and other early analysts did not work in sterile spaces; their offices were filled with books and art and artifacts that gave patients a feel for who this person was. The message I want to convey to my patients through my space is this—*You are welcome here to do the healing work that you need to do. This is a safe place, a sanctuary for the wounded parts of you.*

OTHER SANCTUARIES

I also encourage patients to find other sanctuaries, particularly at difficult times during their therapy. From the age of eleven, I spent time in the small woods near my housing project as a refuge from the family tensions caused by my father's alcoholism. I also escaped to those woods from the humiliations and battles in the playground. During difficult times in my adult life I have gone for long, solo walks in woodland nature preserves. What would I have done during that period of leaving my family if I hadn't had those acres of wooded parkland to take daily walks, meditate and do my self-forgiveness work? I hardly know how I would have come through that time without my wooded sanctuary.

At this stage of life I still treasure my weekly walks in the woods as a retreat from the travails of everyday life. I take some time to sit in meditation and prayer along the way, in some place that beckons me on that particular day. During the year or so that I was recovering from cancer surgery and chemotherapy I hadn't the strength to go for my walks, but I could go outside, sit on my bench and meditate for a little while. Those moments were a godsend, islands of sanctuary during a period of intense physical and mental struggle.

Jesus went into the desert; Buddha sat under the Bodhi tree; Lao-tzu was a master of translating nature's teachings. So many spiritual teachers have left a legacy that points directly to being in nature as a sanctuary and as a pathway to transformation. This has been a theme in my life and work for a long time and I regularly recommend to patients that they, too, seek out some easily accessible place that has personal resonance for them. I encourage them to return again and again to that place, imbuing it with a sense of purpose and sacredness. The chapters on *Self-Forgiveness* and *The Council* give many different examples of ways in which nature can be a refuge during times of deep healing and intense inner work. For some patients this is a new notion, but for many it is more a re-awakening of a long-dormant connection to nature. It always intrigues me how often patients are drawn to a place that recalls for them the salutary effect of a childhood or adolescent relationship with some place in the natural world. They easily realize the wisdom in again seeking sanctuary in nature. I encourage them to make these sojourns in solitude. Because unexpected feelings, such as rage or deep sadness, often arise during these times of healing, even a loving partner or beloved friend can inhibit the cathartic release of emotions that these feelings evoke.

Other places can offer sanctuary as well—oftentimes it is not even necessary to leave home. Jeanne has a spot in our upstairs room that she calls her "cubby." It is simply a mission-style chair tucked in a corner in front of a window. Sometimes she has her morning coffee there or she may do some writing; sometimes she retreats to her cubby simply to have some solitary time and gaze out the window into the woods. It has become over time a place of contemplation for Jeanne. I have patients who make an altar in some corner of their home. This, too, becomes a place of refuge, a place to keep precious objects, burn incense, say prayers and meditate. For some people going into their garden is a form of mini-retreat. Caring for their flowers or vegetables, weeding, puttering or just sitting on the ground provides a time away from ordinary consciousness and into some interior space.

Some patients find sanctuary in church when no one else is there. They describe a feeling of consolation as they sit and pray in a safe and sacred space. This sense of serenity is then carried out of the church and into their lives. One of my patients also talked about how she felt a sense of safety and being emotionally held by her congregation during church services. She especially felt it after the death of her husband. The weekly service became a refuge for her during her grieving.

For other patients, their journal becomes a sanctuary. Especially during the Council process or when someone is dealing with a big issue that is in their consciousness much of the time, I recommend that they write in a journal. It provides a vehicle for processing the inner dialogues that arise and offers a safe place to contemplate the complex mixture of thoughts, feelings and dreams that emerge during psychotherapeutic work. The journal becomes an emotional container—they take what is inside of them and put it "out there." Some of my patients bring their journal to sessions. They may write down some of what I say or our shared insights so that they can refer to it during the week. Others write as if they were talking to me during a session. Often people develop an affectionate attachment to their journal and find it comforting to have this companion on their difficult journey. Some patients, however, are ambivalent about their journal. That was true for Maria.

As I discussed in *The Council* chapter, Maria found it helpful to use a journal as a safe place to bring all her thoughts and feelings during her husband Vinny's cancer diagnosis and treatment. During this time of raw emotion, she felt repeatedly frustrated in her efforts to talk to friends. Although well intentioned, Maria's friends didn't respond to her in ways she felt were helpful. Especially because she felt that some of her feelings were socially unacceptable, our sessions and her journal felt to her like her only safe havens. After a time, however, Maria revealed, with some embarrassment, that she had not been writing for weeks. As we explored this further, Maria acknowledged that she was trying to minimize how much the cancer had taken over their lives. Her journal writing had become a persistent reminder of its impact. When she did not want to think about what the cancer had taken from them, she would forget to write in her journal. This ambivalence continued throughout Maria's Council work. We both came to accept that sometimes the journal was a safe, helpful companion and at other times it was an unwelcome reminder of the physical and emotional impacts of the cancer.

These other places of refuge that I have mentioned become adjuncts to the primary sanctuary—the therapeutic relationship. While the way in which I am talking about this relationship as a safe haven is generally not discussed in our professional training, it is important that we think about the therapeutic experience from our patients' viewpoint. They come to us asking for help at a time of suffering and vulnerability and we ask them, in the service of healing, to do something they rarely do—reveal their innermost thoughts and feelings. Why should they trust us? They've been hurt before when they've been open and vulnerable—why would we be any different? Perhaps as we bring this idea of sanctuary more into our conscious minds and attend to the ways in which we can offer this to our patients—in the feel of our space, in our compassionate presence, in conveying other ideas about providing sanctuary—it registers with them on multiple levels of consciousness that they can take refuge with us for this regular period of time. As that sense of safety grows, our patients respond by allowing us entry deeper into their worlds.

THE SELF AS SANCTUARY

Perhaps the ultimate goal for us all is to become a sanctuary for ourselves, developing a safe psychological place within our own consciousness that we can rely on to be a source of solace, compassion and wise guidance. This is certainly my experience. As therapists it's imperative that we grow into our own inner sense of sanctuary so that we can offer ourselves as models for the kind of relationship that our patients can develop within themselves. By internalizing what they experience with us, instead of wanting to escape from themselves during difficult times, they can learn to look inward toward a safe refuge that is always with them.

As I think about it, the ultimate source of inner sanctuary is our Higher Self. As I age, my relationship with Wiseheart deepens. When I look at the redwood carving of him in my office or imagine his presence, I now call him "my old friend." At times of struggle with patients I look to him. Outside the office I think of him as my daily companion. When my patient Tom regularly says to his Higher Power, Jeremiah, "What do you think, big fella?" I can hear the process of deepening relationship with his Higher Self evolving for him. When my patient Richard tells me about his frequent conversations with his Wise Elder, Father Dan, I sense that same unfolding, deeper connection. As my own relationship with Wiseheart evolves and I witness these similar processes occurring with some patients, I more and more encourage other patients to begin to nurture their own version of that connection. As I feel my own sense of inner sanctuary with Wiseheart deepen, I want the people I love to eventually experience that too.

(10)

RECHARGING

It is 8 a.m. and my first patient walks into the office and begins talking immediately. She is feeling a lot of sadness about the end of her marriage. That tear-filled session ends and after a few minutes the next patient enters to talk about his escalating fears about finding any work to support his family. It's been several months since he lost his job and thus far his search for new work has been unsuccessful. After he leaves I see a woman who had a flashback yesterday of being molested by her uncle when she was ten years old. The final patient of the morning is a man who rants about the unfairness of his life and all the injustice in the world. The office walls reverberate with the energy of his rage. Then it is time for a lunch break, a nap and a return to the office for the afternoon's group of patients. Then there is tomorrow. After that is next week, next month, next year.

Each of my patients needs me to be a compassionate listener, a source of loving-kindness and a carrier of hope. How is it possible for me to be in the energy field of that much suffering each day and then go home and be emotionally available for my partner and our children? As therapists, how do we sustain that level of presence and not become exhausted, overwhelmed, emotionally distant, resentful and numb? This is one of the greatest challenges of our work. Yet it is insufficiently addressed in our training, supervision and the professional literature.

I call this process of taking care of ourselves *recharging*. Being with patients is emotionally and physically draining. It depletes our levels of energy. By recharging I mean the ways that we renew our energy supplies, how we replenish our emotional, physical and spiritual batteries. As therapists we need to acknowledge that this is an issue and not minimize its importance. Each of us must recognize the need to take care of ourselves in ways that fit our unique personalities, our current stage of life and our way of being a therapist. This must be addressed each week, each day, each session.

WE DO NOT TAKE GOOD CARE OF OURSELVES

One of the intriguing questions that I encounter in working with therapists who are supervisees or patients is, "Why don't I take better care of myself?" We are usually good at taking care of the needs of others, yet often remiss in taking good care of our bodies, our emotional needs and our spiritual lives. When I talk about this with therapists they most commonly respond with, "How do I find the time and energy in my busy life to do these things for myself?" Having been there in my own journey, I respect the truth in that response—we're all busy. I also know from personal experience that by *taking* the time to regularly recharge myself, paradoxically, I have *more* energy and *more* time. My usual response to this pleading question is, "It is true that in the busyness of your life it's hard to find the time to do things to take care of yourself. Yet everyone that is important to you—your wife, children, patients and yourself—benefits when you are able to do so. Before we talk about the possible ways you might recharge your batteries, though, can you consider the possibility that you might have some psychological block that gets in the way of taking care of yourself?"

For many of us, the caretaker part of our personalities is overdeveloped and the "taking care of self" part is underdeveloped. Each has its roots in our personal history. Many of us were either consciously or unconsciously drawn to this caretaker profession because it was a role we played in our families. This part of us became overdeveloped because it was a primary source of approval, love and self-esteem. Often from a very young age, sometimes as young as four or five, we were the emotional or physical caretakers of a parent, grandparent or sibling. They needed us to be in that role and rewarded us with praise and other forms of love. Being in that role made us feel good about ourselves. We might have had other members of our family who were viewed as self-absorbed or self-centered. A parent or grandparent may have told us that we were not like the others. In our private thoughts we inflated our self-image with notions of being good or superior and diminished the other family members as bad or inferior. The degree to which this dynamic was operative in our family story is the measure of how much the seemingly simple and good suggestion to take better care of ourselves creates inner havoc.

At one level of consciousness the advice to replenish our worn out batteries makes excellent and rational sense. At other levels of consciousness, the suggestion makes us feel anxious, confused and guilty. To follow it makes us feel as if we are taking a huge risk. If we start to do things to take care of ourself, one part of our personality may begin to criticize and judge us as selfish, while another part may be terrified that we are giving up our most reliable way of obtaining love. It feels like if we take care of ourselves, we will stop taking care of others. If we stop taking care of other people, will they stop loving us? This dilemma is quite profound for many therapists and requires a good amount of time and personal therapy to work through and come to a place of better balance.

MATT

After a full day of seeing patients Matt came home tired and expected to be greeted with a kiss by his wife, Amy. Instead she was upstairs working with their ten-year-old on his homework. She called out to him, "I was in school today for a conference with Tommy's teacher and she suggested he could use some help with math. I didn't have time to make dinner so the kids and I just had scrambled eggs." Annoyed, Matt went into the kitchen to cook a meal for himself and noticed dishes in the sink. Grumbling, he made himself some eggs and cleaned up the leftover dishes. Afterwards he went upstairs and found Amy asleep in bed with their three-year-old daughter. He sighed, closed the bedroom door and decided to turn on the computer. Then he stopped himself.

Six months before, Matt, a psychotherapist in his early forties, had initiated treatment with me because Amy had woken up one night to discover him at the computer surfing porn sites. He was humiliated and ashamed; she was disgusted and wanted to know how long had this been going on. He did not tell her that he would often check these sites on his laptop during his afternoon break, but he did reveal that it had been many months. She insisted that he get help.

As we began our work together, Matt told me that he was feeling very depleted as a therapist. He described an absence of any fun in his life. He rarely spent time with his male friends and was becoming increasingly resentful of weekends filled with household chores. Matt was irritable at home and would become critical of Amy saying to her, "How many men do as much as I do and you don't even appreciate it." Big fights would ensue, ending with Matt and Amy withdrawing from each other. Often Amy would go to bed early saying she was tired. While this gave Matt some needed separate time, it was not good separate time. He was filled with resentment, guilty about starting fights and missing the intimacy with Amy. Matt was spending more and more hours on the computer while she was asleep.

Matt was the youngest of five children. His mother was obese, depressed, and exhausted from raising all those kids. Her own mother had died when she was five and Matt felt that she had never recovered from that loss. "There was a heavy sadness that was always with her," he said with a deep sigh and a beginning tearfulness. Whenever Matt would come home from school his mother would ask him to help her with some housework or to go shopping for dinner and get some cookies or snacks for her. She would always praise him by saying, "What a good boy you are" and contrast him to his older brothers who were always playing sports or hanging out with their friends. She would tell him stories about how difficult her childhood was after her mother's death and how she was sent to live with one of her aunts. Matt's father was seldom home, working overtime as a machinist. Oftentimes he would play poker after work and work on cars with his friends on Saturdays. When he was home, Matt's mother would complain and call his father selfish; they would argue. Matt developed a secret sense of superiority to his father and brothers. He felt that he was "the good boy" and a good young man who was always available and helpful to his mother. He really liked it when she praised him and would tell himself, "I'm not selfish like them." Secretly he was envious that they were having fun.

Because of this background, Matt had a lot of difficulty spending any time away from his wife and kids. He repeatedly turned down invitations to ski or play tennis with his male friends despite his enjoyment of those activities. He loved to sing, but ended his involvement with a local choral group after the birth of his first child. Matt thought that for him to do those things would be "selfish just like my father and brothers, just like other men." He acknowledged to me that this secret sense of superiority was a major source of his self-image and esteem. Initially Matt felt embarrassed and exposed when he told me this. And while it was scary to consider the possibility of letting go of the need to feel superior, it was also liberating. For him, taking care of himself had always equaled being selfish. I helped Matt to understand the difference between those people who are characterologically self-centered and selfish, and people who are able to perform healthy acts of self-love.

As Matt came to understand more deeply the childhood roots of his inability to take care of his physical and emotional needs, he was able to see how he was using the internet porn to fill this void. As we worked through those early issues, Matt was able to share his insights with Amy and they gradually came to a place of forgiveness and deeper intimacy. Time together became a priority. So did time skiing and playing tennis with his male friends. Taking the risk to give up his childhood way of getting love by suppressing his own needs, Matt and his family—as well as his patients—reaped the benefits.

THE DANGER OF ADDICTION

One morning thirty years ago some voice inside me said, "You have to stop doing this." Hung over from a night of drinking with friends, images came into my mind of the silly and embarrassing things I had done. Memories of the drinking episodes of my father and other alcoholic relatives floated into my conscious. I recalled my first internship at Bird S. Coler Hospital in New York where I saw the possible endpoint of years of drinking—brain damage, amputated limbs, incoherent speech. That morning I resolved that from that day forward I would never have more than two drinks in a day. I feel blessed that I have been able to fulfill that contract with myself. It is unusual now for me ever to have more than one drink in a day. Was I an alcoholic? Not yet. Was I well on my way to becoming one? Very possibly. When I look back on that morning I view it as a moment of grace. Some combination of knowing my genetic history and the terrifying imprints of how alcoholism had ravaged the lives of those hospital patients helped me to be receptive to that admonishing and guiding inner voice.

Eighteen years ago I realized that I had a sports addiction. For years, after a day of seeing patients, I would go into the house, have a meal and then join my sons, Mark and Scott, in the family room to watch a couple of hours of sports on TV. On weekend afternoons I would do the same thing—with or without the boys. Depending on the season we would also go to see college basketball games or professional baseball games. If I didn't go with Mark and Scott I went with friends. During those years I just told myself *this is what men do*. Like all addicts I had good rationalizations.

It wasn't until after my divorce and Jeanne and I were living together that I really began to look at this pattern and consider why I had been watching so many hours of sports. My first marriage, as far as I was concerned, was quite good, better than most. Yet I did not allow myself to reflect on why I was spending that time with sports rather than with my wife. I was in denial about my own needs for a deeper level of emotional intimacy and physical affection. The contrast of my relationship with Jeanne helped me to understand what was missing and how my addiction to sports was an attempt to fill that void.

Not wanting to continue this earlier pattern, I took a beautiful quilt that a patient had given me at our last session and used it to cover the television. This was my symbolic gesture to demonstrate that I would no longer allow the TV screen to be a centerpiece of my life. It kept me mindful of my commitment to remaining aware of the slippery slope of addiction. Eighteen years down the road, the quilt still covers the TV and I still watch sports. Now, however, I maintain a better balance and watching sports is only a small part of how I spend my time. Not wanting to deprive myself totally of something that gives me pleasure and provides a way of connecting with my sons and with friends, I never abstain altogether. I have found a path of recovery from my addiction that works for me—most of the time. Occasionally during college basketball season I will feel the seductive pull of the addictive trance and find myself watching games two or three days in a row. When that happens I abstain for a while. It usually is a week or more before the quilt comes off the TV again. But those seductive episodes are now rare.

I do allow myself a binge each year during March Madness when I spend several days in New York watching college basketball. But this time has always been partly about spending time with Mark and Scott and some friends. Since my experience with cancer, this time in New York has evolved into a mini vacation for myself, one part of which is watching basketball and other parts that involve going to art galleries and museums, listening to jazz, eating good food and being with friends. There are a couple of days where I still might see three or four games in a day and I still compete with my sons in a basketball pool. At the end of it all, I feel satiated with pleasure—and a little hung over. I eagerly look forward to regaining the balance in my life.

It is this personal history of my own scrapes with addictions that helps me to feel compassionate with Matt's struggles. My experience has also prodded me to reflect on the danger of addictions for therapists in general.

I think that there are two primary reasons why therapists are prone to addictions. The first has to do with the amount of human suffering that we are exposed to. We are trying to be open-hearted, compassionate human beings. Yet, to be continually in the energy field of tremendous emotional struggle and pain every day is more than our small hearts can contain. It is understandable that we become emotionally disconnected from patients during sessions. It is understandable why the notion of maintaining a professional emotional distance is so appealing. It is also understandable that we unconsciously seek out substances or activities that will help to numb us so that we feel less of the overwhelming pain. Like other addicts, we are trying to disconnect from unwanted feelings and fill some psychological or spiritual emptiness. Because we often are not good at taking care of ourselves there will be something missing, some hole that we try to fill with the addiction. There is an absence or insufficiency of something that we need—fun, connection to friends, intimacy with a partner, a sense of purpose or meaning, a feeling of community or a relationship with God. Addressing these needs and attending to the ways in which we need recharging can prevent us from falling into addictive patterns.

PATHWAYS

From my perspective, one of the essential ways for us to recharge is to find time for solitude—away from every person on the planet who has any emotional need for us. Because of the nature of our work and the caretaker pattern that so many of us are up against, we are particularly attuned to the needs of others. As a result whenever we are with someone we love, we are usually wondering: *Is she having a good time? What does he want to do? Is she doing this just to please me? Is he tired of this?* Solitary time provides an opportunity to focus only on our needs.

Every week I take a two-hour walk in some local nature place. I treasure this solo time in which I am accessible to no one but myself. I am passionate about jazz and college basketball, and as I just described, periodically I go to a concert or game by myself. One of the greatest pleasures in my life is eating good, nourishing food. At least once each week I go to a restaurant for lunch by myself. I imagine that the chef is taking care of only me. Several times a week, I prepare meals for myself while Jeanne is working and think about how I am taking care of someone I love—me! I never do any work or any thinking related to work while preparing or enjoying these meals. Each of these solitary experiences nourishes a part of me.

We all need to learn what solitary activity recharges us. Jeanne has a studio where she paints, works with mosaic tiles or wood or some other creative medium. This time of play and creativity is an essential source of nurturing for her. There is no phone or anything that connects her to the outside world in this studio space. She also spends many solo hours in her flower garden digging, planting, transplanting and mulching. When she is gardening it is as if she is in a trance, just her and the plants. I know another therapist who takes rides on his motorcycle, one who rides her horse, others who take long runs or bicycle rides, knit or compose songs. Because our work is so sedentary and because we can carry some of the emotional energy of our patients in our bodies, I think that it is especially valuable to have a recharging activity that involves physical movement. Each of these activities is nourishing for that particular therapist.

It is also essential to find ways of recharging ourselves that involve doing something playful with others. So many hours of our work are involved with patients who are suffering as they deal with the serious issues of their lives. We need to counterbalance this time with fun activities with playmates. For some therapists this involves being in community theater. Others like hiking or biking with a group. For others it may be watching Sunday afternoon football, having a weekly poker game, jamming with a band or singing with a choral group. The common denominator is being with people who share a similar passion. It is important in our personal therapy to work through whatever blocks we may have to taking solo time or being playful so we can seek out the activities that will replenish us and help sustain our work.

As we become aware of our need for separate time and play time, one of the biggest challenges is how to express to loved ones our need for recharging time. Oftentimes a partner feels rejected or abandoned when we go off alone or to play with friends. What I've learned over time to say is, "It's not that I want to be away from *you*, but that I need to be with *me*. I'm not rejecting *you*; I'm taking care of *me*. When I get time to recharge my batteries you get more of me. If I take this time for me, I will have more to give to you and our relationship." From my experience, our loved ones are usually quite receptive to this way of explaining what we are doing. However, because most people have had experiences where someone really did want to be away from them, it will take repeated explanations until it sinks in that what we are doing is different from those others. Over time Jeanne and I have deepened our understanding of just how important separate time is and how much our relationship benefits when we are both getting regular time to recharge.

DURING SESSIONS

Hour after hour, day after day, week after week we are exposed to human suffering. Our patients need us to be with them in their pain and struggle. They need to feel our empathy and caring. How can we do that day in and day out and not become overwhelmed or retreat into a state of professional distance to protect our hearts? Recharging ourselves in our time away from the work is certainly necessary, but what about during sessions? What can we do while we are with our patients?

How we answer those questions will depend on how we view what goes on in therapy and our own cosmology. One viewpoint that I find helpful to consider is that part of what occurs in the therapeutic relationship is an exchange of energy. A patient enters our office in a depressed, anxious, depleted, angry or confused energy state. Hopefully, we are in a more harmonious, grounded energy state of relative equilibrium. The patient, in a state of imbalance, is seeking some level of equilibrium, and in the process some of their negative emotional energy enters into the energy field of our consciousness. The more open-hearted we are, the more this exchange seems to occur. If at this moment, you doubt this happens, think back to the last time that you were with a highly anxious person. After a while didn't you, too, start to feel anxious? Do you remember how weighted down and heavy you felt when the office space was filled with the sadness of a grieving patient? Recall the electrical charge that seemed to reverberate in the room when someone was raging and how your body seemed subtly to recoil from them. Think back to those times when patients have left your office feeling better and somehow you felt worse. They seemed to be lighter, less depressed, fearful or angry and you felt down, anxious, tired or irritable. Perhaps at those moments, because you were open-hearted and receptive, some of their charged emotions or energy entered into your own field of consciousness and remained there. Then the next patient enters. What now often happens is that we start to close down in order to ward off the negative energy of the next patient. Or the feeling states start to accumulate over several hours. We become more and more tired/depleted/distant as the morning or evening continues. We have less available energy for the third or fourth patient. We are becoming less and less optimally present with each subsequent session. Gradually we lose our state of balance.

In order to release these energy states from my field of consciousness and to continually restore my equilibrium, I have developed ways of recharging during sessions that are quite effective for me. I use focused imagery and deep breathing while with my patients. Throughout the office I have reminders of the activities that recharge me. My weekly sojourns walking in the woods among the trees replenish me, and so diagonally across from my chair I have hanging a large poster of a giant redwood. For me, that huge tree symbolizes great strength and endurance. It reminds me of how replenished I feel among the trees. When

I am with a patient in a depleted or depressed feeling state, I glance at the redwood and imagine what it feels like to be that titan. I then breathe quietly into my belly, imagining myself taking in that strength. As I exhale gently through my mouth, I imagine the patient's negative emotional energy leaving my field of consciousness. I continue this cyclical breathing while I am listening, staying fully present and considering how I might respond.

When I am with a patient who is highly anxious or fearful, I glance at the Taoist painting of a man in a boat on a lake that hangs on the wall behind the patient's chair and it helps me to remember the sense of tranquility I feel when I sit in meditation at the edge of a nearby beaver pond. Breathing in, I take in the peaceful energy the painting symbolizes. Breathing out, I imagine myself letting go of the anxious energy emanating from the patient.

The redwood poster is also helpful when I am in the presence of a patient's anger. I think of the many storms that the ancient tree has weathered. Through raging storms its top just sways with the wind while its trunk remains solidly rooted. Even though it has been hit by lightning many times, the core of the redwood is unaffected and the tree continues to grow. During the patient's outburst of anger I will glance at the redwood, remember those qualities and breathe. In this way I can connect to those qualities within myself and continue to be an open-hearted person.

I also feel that I am not alone in doing this work. If I had to consider that it is only my little self or small heart that is present to the patient, then the work would be too daunting. How could my small human heart cope with the amount of sadness, terror, despair, rage, depletion and confusion that I witness? However, I believe that my Higher Self is also present to assist and guide me. From my perspective, that part of my personality is the source of my deepest wisdom, the container of my knowledge of the human psyche, and a well of great compassion that I can tap into at any moment. As I have said before, I have named this aspect of my nature *Wiseheart*. On the floor of my office, in a corner next to the patient's chair, I have an iconic image of this wise old man carved in redwood. Whenever I feel the need for assistance from my Higher Self—which is often—I glance at this totem for a moment, inhale deeply into my belly and internally say, *Help me to help her*. I then exhale, letting go of any feelings of being overwhelmed and helpless. In this way I am trying to create an opening in my consciousness so I may be receptive to the assistance of my Higher Self. I consider, too, that the Higher Self of the patient is also present in the room, a reservoir of their own inner wisdom available to assist us in the therapeutic process. Periodically when I feel clueless about what to say or uncertain about what is happening in the therapy process at that moment, I will glance above the head of the patient and imagine myself in dialogue with their Higher Self saying, *Please help her to be open to whatever is possible in her healing process today.*

We have all been influenced by particular teachers or guides that we have either known personally, have heard speak or whose writings we have read. They have influenced our thinking and the ways we do our work. I think it is possible to access these teachers for assistance during sessions. Sometimes I am accessing memories of what I have learned from their teachings and methods of working, or I might imagine what it was like to be in their presence. Other times, I feel that I am connecting to their actual consciousness—perhaps on the level of collective consciousness—as something that is eternal and available to me. While many teachers have influenced me, the two most significant carriers for me of the wisdom of the heart are Jesus and Buddha. In my office I have small statues of each of them as iconic reminders of this wisdom. Periodically during sessions I will look at these figures and breathe deeply, imagining myself opening to them as sources of compassionate wisdom and as hearts much larger than mine. With my out-breath I imagine myself letting go of my own doubts and fears. I feel less alone in these moments and assisted by something greater than myself.

Recharging in these ways each day that I do my work enables me to maintain an open-hearted presence with my patients for hours and not feel depleted. I encourage you to adapt these approaches in ways that fit your unique psychological and spiritual perspectives and to explore other pathways that might be of help in recharging during sessions.

(11)

ANAM CARA

My grandparents were Irish immigrants, my parents, first-generation Irish. In closing this book I want to return to my Celtic roots to further expand the way we view our work as psychotherapists. The Celtic tradition offers us the notion of *anam cara*. In Gaelic the word *anam* means soul and *cara* is a word for friend. Throughout this work I have advocated for each of us to become a synthesis of well-trained professional and loving human being. In this brief final chapter, I am encouraging us to be a particular kind of friend for our patients—a friend of their souls. Interestingly, in earlier Celtic history, the *anam cara* was a teacher or spiritual guide—we might say the psychotherapists of their era.

In reflecting on the word *anam* it is not my intention to engage in an ontological discussion of the notion of "soul." That conversation is well beyond the scope of this book. Suffice it to say that what I mean by soul in this context is the essential nature of the person. If you observe young children, you will see that clues to their essence are available to the attentive eye from a very early time. In the leather sleeve of my appointment book, I carry individual pictures of my sons, Mark and Scott—who are now thirty-nine and thirty-six—when they were three-year-olds. One of the reasons I treasure these early photos is that they capture something of the souls—the essence—of my sons. Observing them as adult men,

I now witness the full flowering of the seeds of their essential natures, aspects of their unique characters, that were present at age three. It is this hard-to-describe facet of who they are that the Celts call *anam*. In an attempt to find another way of describing soul, I sometimes refer to these characteristics of their essential natures as their "Markness" and "Scottness."

Like my sons, for most of my patients, their essential nature was probably out in the world to some degree when they were young. Now their souls are in hiding most of the time. Perhaps we get a periodic, brief glimpse of their souls or see aspects of their original nature in some distortion of their more innocent form. For the most part, however, the souls of our patients have been neglected, abused or wounded, treated with apathy or disrespect. And so they remain in hiding.

A primary goal of a heart-centered approach to psychotherapy is to invite the soul to come out again—to become free to explore its potential and evolve into a full fruition of its possibilities. From my experience, what the souls of my patients most respond to is not rational insights or cognitive techniques, but compassionate presence and acts of loving-kindness.

Cara refers to a particular kind of friendship. It is not an acquaintance or a friend with whom we connect on superficial levels. *Cara* is the kind of friend who enters the "deep within" with us and treats what he or she meets there with the respectful reverence of someone who knows they are in sacred territory. A *cara* invites the soul to come out through encouragement, affection, celebrations and moments of loving challenge that carry the message "you are valued" and "I am here to help you become more fully who you can be." He or she is the kind of friend who is extending a welcoming hand to the multiple parts of that essential nature, conveying the message that all of you can feel *at home* with me.

Earlier in my practice my patients would say that it felt to them like I was their friend, but that it was a particular kind of friendship that was unfamiliar to them. It didn't fit into any category of friendship that they knew. How could they be friends with someone they saw in this confined space for less than an hour a week? And whom they paid? When they would describe this to me I would often feel awkward or feel that maybe something unprofessional was happening. Perhaps I had inadvertently overstepped some boundary. In those days, when I attempted to describe to my patients what I thought was occurring, I would often stumble around trying to find adequate words. It was usually an uncomfortable territory for both of us.

I would wager that for most of the readers of this book, there was no mention in their training that one of the facets of being a therapist could be to become a friend of the souls of their patients. Certainly that was not part of my training. So when these feelings of some kind of friendship arose in the early years of my work, I felt that I, or perhaps my patient, was doing something wrong. I pathologized it. And yet, if I had really considered the etymology of the word *psychotherapist*, that possible meaning of the word might have occurred to me.

My interest in etymology started fifty years ago when my professors of Greek, Latin, and English literature all stressed that, whenever someone wanted to deeply understand the meaning of a word, it was essential to begin the search by looking at its origins. Etymologically, *psychotherapy* is a synthesis of the Greek words *psyche* and *therapeia* or *therapon*. The primary meaning of *psyche* is soul; *therapeia* is healing; *therapon* is attendant. So in its original meaning the quality of being a psychotherapist is to be a healer or attendant to the souls of our patients. That concept is certainly aligned with the Celtic notion of *anam cara*. Yet, with the exception, perhaps, of the Jungian and Psychosynthesis theories of psychotherapy, this perspective was not talked about openly in traditional training. Rather, what was emphasized was the subconscious and unconscious as the realms in which the suppressed and repressed parts of the self exist. We were not taught that, coexisting in that subterranean world, is the secret and sacred realm of the soul—our unique essence—awaiting an invitation to come out and be free again.

The notion of *anam cara* has become very helpful to me in understanding what my patients and I have been experiencing together. It gives me language to describe a relationship that doesn't fit easily into another category. A Buddhist might use the term *Kalyana-mitra* or "noble friend" to describe this kind of friendship. Or, as I have said elsewhere in this book, the word *agape* also describes well this kind of loving presence. For me personally, I love that the term *anam cara* comes from my Irish roots and, frankly, I simply like the sound of the words. So now, when some of my patients end sessions by saying, "See you next week, my friend," or sometimes, "I love you, my friend" I am more easily able to take in their affection for me as a soul friend.

As psychotherapists, we are an eclectic group of individuals practicing from diverse theoretical perspectives and personal worldviews. It is my hope that what I have come to know over almost forty years of doing this work provides guidance and a path for other therapists to actively and directly engage in a more heart-centered approach with their patients, using our minds *and* our hearts to express love and caring in ways that fit with our essential natures and that are always in the best interest of our patients.

INDEX

ABOUT THE AUTHOR

William P. Ryan, PhD, has been a psychologist in private practice for more than thirty-five years. He has taught college at both undergraduate and graduate levels and been a consultant in drug prevention, agencies for children and law enforcement. In addition, he has published three books: coauthor of *Love Blocks: Breaking the Patterns that Undermine Relationships* (Viking 1989); coauthor of *In the Woods, At the Water: Healing Journeys Into Nature* (Temenos Press 1999); and author of *The Bench, The Council and The Prayer* (Temenos Press 2002).

After many years of working in suburban Huntington, New York, Bill is enjoying semi-retirement and small-town life at his brookside cottage in Ashfield, Massachusetts. The local nature preserves provide many opportunities for contemplative saunters in the woods. At the age of sixty, for the first time in his life, Bill decided to learn to play a musical instrument—folk harp. Nine years later the sense of musical competence gained from practicing at home and periodically playing out has deeply enriched this stage of his life.

Lightning Source UK Ltd.
Milton Keynes UK
UKHW040206080620
364476UK00025B/794

9 781442 235120